THE POP-UP GYM

JON DENORIS

HOW TO KEEP FIT WHEREVER YOU ARE

BLOOMSBURY

LONDON · NEW DELHI · NEW YORK · SYDNEY

Dedication

To my mum and dad,
for allowing me to make my own choices.

Published 2014 by Bloomsbury Publishing Plc,
50 Bedford Square, London WC1B 3DP

www.bloomsbury.com

Bloomsbury is a trade mark of Bloomsbury Publishing Plc

Copyright © 2014 text by Jon Denoris
Copyright © 2014 photographs Gerard Brown
Copyright © 2014 photographs is held by the individual photographers
see credits on page 192

The right of Jon Denoris to be identified as the author of this work
has been asserted by him in accordance with the Copyright,
Designs and Patents Act 1988.

ISBN (print) 978-1-4081-9632-8
ISBN (epub) 978-1-4729-0059-3

A CIP catalogue record for this book is available from the British Library

This book is produced using paper that is made from wood
grown in managed sustainable forests. It is natural, renewable
and recyclable. The logging and manufacturing processes conform
to the environmental regulations of the country of origin.

Design: Nicola Liddiard, Nimbus Design

Printed in China by C & C Offset Printing Co Ltd

10 9 8 7 6 5 4 3 2 1

NOTE

Whilst every effort has been made to ensure that the
content of this book is as technically accurate and as
sound as possible, neither the authors nor the publishers
can accept responsibility for any injury or loss sustained
as a result of the use of this material.

Contents

Foreword by Jo Wood **5**

Introduction Get yourself fit, for free, for life, forever! **6**

Chapter 1 The 15 benefits of the Pop-up Gym **10**

Chapter 2 Removing the barriers to exercising **18**

Chapter 3 Fitting exercise into your lifestyle **24**

Chapter 4 Setting benchmarks **32**

Chapter 5 Getting and staying motivated **46**

Chapter 6 Getting and staying supple **56**

Chapter 7 The exercises: 55 ways to total fitness **66**

Chapter 8 Warm-up, cool down **126**

Chapter 9 The workouts **134**

Chapter 10 Quick fixes and feats of strength **158**

Chapter 11 Clever strategies for fat loss **164**

The next six months **172**

References **174**

Index **175**

Acknowledgments **176**

'Physical culture is
The Greatest Need of the Day'

Dr Davey, President of The British Medical Association, 1907

'We know that more than 60 per cent
of adults are not active enough.'

Professor Dame Sally Davies, Chief Medical Officer, 2011

'Definition of insanity: doing the same
thing over and over again,
and expecting a different result.'

Albert Einstein

Foreword

The day I met Jon was fate ... destiny ... I noticed Club 51 as I pulled over on Cavendish Street to take a call. I Googled him to find out some more details and the rest is history. That was over three years ago and I have honestly never looked back.

Jon really is the whole package and his holistic approach to fitness, combining restoration, nutrition and movement together means he takes into account all different elements of fitness, inclusive of your ideas. My passion for an organic lifestyle and his knowledge has led to countless chats about the benefits of Omega 3 oils, coconut oil and much more. His approach is all about simplifying things to create and maintain a long-lasting healthy lifestyle.

With his background in psychology and behaviour change, Jon understands how to help people in the public eye deal with the pressures that go with this type of life while his targeted approach is perfect for busy people. Jon is not just one of the best fitness trainers I have ever had but also the best educator and motivator to make sure you get the best out of your body. There are so many times he has pushed me beyond limits I didn't even realise I could reach with my fitness.

The Pop-up Gym will inspire you to get up and train anywhere, whether it's at home or on the go and is perfect for busy people who don't have a lot of time to go into a gym and train regularly. Thanks to Jon, I am the fittest I have ever been and his book is essential reading to anyone who wants to achieve the same.

Get fit for life, for free, forever!

I'm going to show you how you can become fitter and healthier with a minimum of fuss. You won't have to go to a gym, you won't have to spend a lot of money on equipment, and this won't take up a lot of your time. In fact, the whole fitness programme I have devised has been designed with busy people in mind. Does all this sound too good to be true? It is anything but that.

I've always been mad about fitness. As a teenager I was obsessed with sports and fitness of all kinds and tried any fitness routine I could find, I travelled two hours each way to learn Kung Fu (even though the teacher didn't say a word to me for the first year). I read every magazine, and experimented with different diets.

I'd spend hours watching and copying my dad do his workout with chest expanders: he used anything he could get hold of from around the house and was a fan of all the old bodybuilders and physical culturists. He told me stories of growing up in Africa, where he would use 'elephant tusks' to train with because that's all they had (I still believe him!). The original Pop-up Gym!!

In more recent years, I have been lucky enough to coach some of the most successful and powerful people from the worlds of business, politics, sport and entertainment, and it is through this work that my idea of The Pop-up Gym was born.

This particular group of clients share more in common than you would think. Results driven, time poor and often managing multiple diaries across multiple time zones, they can't afford to waste any effort. Whether in a confined space, on the set of a movie, or in their hotel room, I required a creative approach to exercise, flexible, without the use of sophisticated gym equipment yet ruthlessly effective. The result of this is the Pop-up Gym.

My exercises and routines will improve your physical and mental shape. In particular, functional strength, cardiovascular health and whole body flexibility, will all noticeably improve. All common areas of fitness which new clients tell me they have lost.

Performing these exercises will make you less susceptible to back strain, and less likely to have problems with the key postural muscles of your lower body. Finally, the exercises will develop the body's core strength, and help to strip away fat around the middle. In so doing they will lead to significant, but safe, weight loss. In short, the exercises are holistic, for they strengthen the entire body.

After only six weeks of practising these exercises you will experience a visible improvement in your overall shape and a noticeable difference in your body composition and flexibility. Functional movements such as lifting bags and luggage, climbing stairs or stretching down will start to feel easier.

Three months later you will feel as if you have a new body. In a sense you will. So these exercises have a real, practical, everyday value, as well as enabling you, the exerciser to lose weight (body fat) and look better.

Some of my exercises draw inspiration from the Victorian ideals of physical culture. Others have been specially developed more recently, and all have been develop to work together in my plan. What they all have in common – especially the exercise routines – is that they are backed by the latest sports science. As a sports scientist with my own gym, and with more than 20,000 hours' experience of helping clients to get fit, I have had plenty of opportunity to experiment and know what works and what doesn't. Some of my older clients have made tremendous strides in their health and fitness by performing these exercises. I have graded the exercises and the routines, so that anyone embarking on them for the first time will be able to progress through them at their own pace.

Of the 15 major benefits of this book, about half are lifestyle rather than physical. When you undertake these exercises you will find that you have more energy, sleep better, experience greater creativity, enhanced mental capacity, reduced stress and all-round resilience. This is no accident. The exercise routines have been deliberately designed to produce these results.

The book deals with all the usual difficulties that most people have when they think about exercising; all those reasons why they can't begin and later why they can't continue. I have developed a strategy for every difficulty, and am adamant that we should all think about our health first.

'Prioritise your health or it will prioritise you.'

To be really effective fitness training has to be backed up by good nutrition. Whilst a full nutrition chapter was beyond the scope of this book, I hope you will find the chapter on 'clever strategies for fat loss' insightful as many of my clients have. The techniques are designed to be implemented into your lifestyle to accelerate the fat burning process and help you become leaner.

Fun is a word on the lips of many of my most famous clients, who include entertainers, sportsmen and sportswomen, business executives, lawyers and politicians. As a result of performing these exercises they have all made amazing changes to their health, fitness and lives. Now you can too with The Pop-up Gym.

What this book will do for you

Chapter 1

The 15 benefits
of the Pop-up Gym

You will get many benefits from this programme. It will improve your health and all-round fitness, and make you calmer in your everyday life, better able to navigate the pressures and stresses that we all face today. If you perform this workout regularly it is likely to enhance your whole being. It might even make you happier.

1. YOU'LL LOOK LEANER, AND MAYBE EVEN A LITTLE YOUNGER!
HERE'S HOW

The exercises will gradually reduce the surplus weight around your stomach; they will increase your muscle to fat ratio; and they'll strengthen your core. Your body will become leaner as a result, you'll feel more able to play sport and you'll look better too. Other people will notice that you look more athletic.

Some of my older clients have taken up sport again, after years of a sedentary life, having followed these exercises. Unless you have specific medical concerns, there is no reason why you too can't achieve that.

2. YOU'LL RAISE YOUR METABOLIC RATE HOW?

All exercise has a tendency to drive up our metabolic rate, but the more intense the exercise, the stronger is the increase in metabolism. As you progress through the routines in the book you will find they have been specially designed to drive up your metabolism, using a mechanism known as EPOC.

EPOC stands for 'excess post-exercise oxygen consumption'. It is also known as 'exercise afterburn', because research has shown that the body uses up extra calories after a burst of high intensity exercise in order to return to its pre-exercise state.

According to the latest research, high intensity circuit training, such as the more advanced routines in this book, can increase resting metabolic rate by 100Kcals per day. That is in addition to the high number of calories that will have been expended by the exercises themselves. So by taking advantage of this mechanism it is possible to increase post-exercise oxygen consumption in order to achieve greater calorie burn. That in turn will result in more effective weight loss.

3. YOU'LL STRENGTHEN YOUR BONES AND JOINTS HOW WILL THAT HAPPEN?

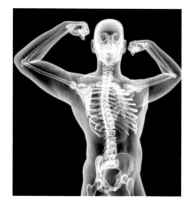

Exercising in itself helps to maintain bone density and joint mobility. Research into physiology and ageing in a number of countries has shown this to be the case. But exercising can do something else. One of the reasons why so many of us complain about pain in our bodies, including our bones, is that the muscles supporting our bone structure have weakened and deteriorated: this is known as sarcopenia by exercise scientists. That's another reason why undertaking the exercises in this book is so valuable. It will give you back some of the muscle strength that you have lost.

So, if you perform the exercises in these workouts, you will strengthen your general musculature, you will maintain your bone density and you'll improve your overall flexibility. What that means is that your quality of life will also improve. Carrying out tasks like walking upstairs with a heavy bag, or reaching out to pick something up will become easier.

4. YOU WILL FIND IT EASIER TO MAINTAIN A HEALTHY WEIGHT HOW?

Taking regular exercise helps to maintain a healthy weight, while short bursts of intense exercise can help to reduce it.

The Pop-up Gym will enable you to reach your ideal weight and maintain it. If you practise the exercises in the workout you should be able to keep to your ideal weight at whatever age you are.

5. YOU'LL BE BETTER ABLE TO CONTROL BLOOD SUGAR LEVELS HOW?

Taking regular exercise can help to lessen the risk of getting diabetes by up to 50 per cent. If you already have type II diabetes, exercise can still be useful because it will help to manage it. Diabetes is thought by many health professionals to be the next major health epidemic, a ticking health time bomb. Exercise and particularly resistance exercise can help the body become more sensitive to insulin thus helping you to control blood sugar more effectively.

Diabetes is thought by many health professionals to be the next major health epidemic, a ticking time bomb ...

6. YOU'LL HAVE A HEALTHIER HEART HOW?

Exercise enables the heart to function more effectively. It helps to reduce the risk of coronary heart disease, to control and regulate blood pressure efficiently and to improve blood lipid (i.e., fat) profiles.

Taking regular exercise with The Pop-up Gym will strengthen your heart and will improve its overall functioning. Whilst the evidence and research around high cholesterol levels is evolving, control of blood lipids via exercise has been shown to contribute to a healthier heart.

7. YOU'LL DEVELOP GREATER INNER STRENGTH, AND FEEL BETTER IN YOUR WHOLE SELF HOW?

More and more research is showing that regular physical exercise enlivens our bodies and makes us feel good, it stimulates the central nervous system which increases the transport of oxygen to the brain as well as cerebral metabolic activity of various neurotransmitters including dopamine, serotonin, norepinephrine, acetylcholin and of course endorphins. The various different types of exercise can have the effect of raising our spirits, making us feel calmer, more grounded, more present to ourselves and others. In short, it strengthens our well-being. That in turn helps us to deal with stress, which we will look at in more detail later.

8. YOU'LL HAVE MORE ENERGY HOW?

The cutting-edge exercise and lifestyle strategies that I have created will dramatically increase your energy levels. If you carry these out regularly you will soon discover that your natural day to day levels of energy are higher than they used to be. You won't just feel on a high for a short time after the exercises, you will find that you have more energy most of the time. Your overall energy level will have made a step change.

Doing the exercise routines in the Pop-up Gym will significantly improve your whole life in a number of ways.

9. YOU'LL INCREASE YOUR CAPACITY TO TOLERATE STRESS
HOW WILL THESE EXERCISES ACHIEVE THAT?

Firstly, by giving you greater energy (see above), the exercise routines will make it easier for your body to tolerate stress and at higher levels than you are probably capable of right now. This is a very different stress strategy from those usually advocated. Most stress reduction regimes focus on reducing the stress triggers are around you, but that isn't always possible. If you work in a difficult environment, changing that environment may not be feasible, and if your journey to and from work is a stressor it is likely that you won't be able to change that either. Living at a higher energy level, which is what these exercises will enable you to do, will make you less susceptible to stress, and also better able to rise above it when you sense that it is starting to have an impact on you. My clients from business and politics call this building 'resilience'; I call it making them battleproof!

The second reason why this programme will help you to cope better with stress is that my exercise techniques will help your body to fight the stress hormone cortisol. Cortisol is a product of chronic stress that can lead to depression and possibly even dementia. The release of cortisol into the body also leads to fat being stored around the waist. The exercises in the workout catalyse the production of proteins that will provide an outlet for the damage caused by cortisol, and therefore delay the onset of depression, dementia and weight gain around the middle of the body.

10. YOU'LL SHARPEN YOUR MENTAL PROCESSES
HOW IS THAT POSSIBLE?

There is a growing body of research that shows how specific types of training can make us smarter, more alert, more creative, more focused and even more competitive. I have incorporated these research findings into the exercise routines here. You may not see a difference in yourself straightaway, but within a few weeks you really should start to see a noticeable improvement in your mental alertness and creativity.

11. THESE ROUTINES WILL HELP TO LIFT YOUR MOOD HOW?

Research at Duke University in the US, has shown that exercise can lift a person's mood. In a well-respected, landmark study a team of researchers compared the efficacy of exercise versus the anti-depressant, Zoloft. Their conclusions, published in the so-called SMILE study, showed that exercise was at least as effective as the drug in helping people with mild depression. I have incorporated the exercise techniques mentioned in their study into The Pop-up Gym.

12. YOU'LL IMPROVE YOUR 'EXECUTIVE FUNCTIONING.'
HOW WILL THAT HAPPEN?

Executive functioning relates to a part of the brain that is responsible for planning, organising and multi-tasking (or juggling). The reason why exercise affects the brain in this way is primarily twofold. First, exercise induces increased blood flow to the brain which means that it is receiving more oxygen, and other essential nutrients for brain functioning. Second, exercise benefits the brain because it also increases levels of a protein known as BDNF (brain derived neurotropic factor). BDNF encourages growth and communication between the brain cells.

Research has also shown that if you combine exercise with certain types of music that stimulate the BDNF protein even more. Examples include music by Vivaldi and Mozart.

13. YOU'LL IMPROVE THE QUALITY OF YOUR SLEEP WHY?

Poor sleep is often the result of anxiety and stress. Exercise has a
tendency to reduce stress. But exercise at the right time can have
another effect. For example, exercising in the morning may be the
most beneficial time for you if you find it difficult to get to sleep. The
exercise will have helped to rebalance your circadian rhythms. For more
information on better, more restful sleep go to **www.popupgym.co.uk**

14. YOU'LL BOOST YOUR IMMUNE SYSTEM HOW?

Moderate activity pushes up the production of your T cells. T cells attack
bacteria, viruses and can even reduce the risk of some type of cancers.
So by performing my exercise routines you will be strengthening yourself
against colds, flu, viruses and you will be less likely to develop certain
kinds of cancers. For example, research has shown that physically
active people have a 50 per cent lower risk of developing colon cancer.
Ensuring that you do not overdo things is critical to this too, whilst the
routines here are challenging, you must balance periods of high intensity
and effort with lower intensity, recovery periods. This interval based
approach to fitness is one of the keys to The Pop-up Gym and what makes
it so successful.

15. YOU'LL ENHANCE AND LENGTHEN YOUR LIFE

All my experience of working with clients has shown me that performing
these exercises will improve the quality of your life. You will become a
more positive person, and you will have more 'joie de vivre.' You are likely
to live longer too. I have clients whom I first knew in their 60s, who as a
result of these exercises are fitter and living happier, healthier lives well
into their next decade and beyond. Believe me, these exercises do work.

Chapter 2
Removing the barriers to exercising

No more excuses

If you're browsing this book or if you've gone and bought it you may still have concerns, doubts, worries even. Getting back into shape might seem a bit daunting. Or you might be living a stressful life and feel tired a lot of the time. Or you may be thinking, 'where am I going to find the time to do all these exercises?'

If any of this sounds familiar, you are not alone. Almost every new client I meet has a list of reasons why they haven't been exercising. My first job is to show them how those reasons can be overcome. I help them to see how the obstacles that seem overwhelming can be surmounted. And in every case they are solved. You too can find a way around the barriers to taking exercise. I will show you how.

Below are some of the most common barriers to getting fit:

1. I HAVE SO LITTLE TIME

This is the most frequent barrier that I come across. That is true even in my fitness studio, where clients have paid me to help them get fit. They, probably like you, are living very busy, often time-pressured lives, and they know all too well the pull of distraction from other people, urgent demands and other things to do.

For them, as for you, I have two answers:

• Take care of yourself now or your lack of care will haunt you
  in years to come.

• Prioritise your health before it prioritises you.

I have met so many people who in their 20s, 30s, 40s, 50s, have not made their health a priority, and who in later years have paid the price. Some of them have come to see me with back pain, heart problems or diabetes, which they could have avoided if only they had taken more care of themselves.

- Fit your exercise in between other activities, and break your exercising down into small chunks of time.

- The exercises in this book have been deliberately designed so that they can be undertaken in short snatches of time.

Don't think of exercise as something that is totally separate from the rest of your life. With a little thought and imagination you can infuse many of your ordinary activities with some exercise, that is, you can adapt them to include some exercise.

2. I'M TOO TIRED WHEN I COME HOME FROM WORK

Taking exercise will actually give you more energy. After exercise you will almost certainly be more awake, have more energy and feel less tired. You become more productive.

The secret is to be patient and not to expect to do everything perfectly first time around. If your body is not used to being physically active you may need to reacquaint yourself with exercise gradually. Take the exercises in small steps. It is far better to do a little exercise regularly then none at all.

Taking exercise is not just a physical activity; it has a psychological aspect too. As you become accustomed to it and more confident about what you can do, you will look forward to it more. The thought of exercise will raise your spirits.

Long-term, the habitual practice of exercising will give you much more energy, by improving your sleep and by raising your metabolism.

3. I'M TOO OLD FOR EXERCISE NOW

It really is never too late to take up exercise again. I have worked with beginners who were in their 60s and even their 70s, when they first came to see me. Over time they were able to build up strength and improve their agility.

Many of us tend to think that exercise really is for the young, and that after a certain age there is not much point in exercising, because it won't have much of an impact on us. We believe that the body has become set in its ways and that there is little that we can do to improve it. That is completely mistaken. New scientific research is showing us that the body – and indeed the mind – is much more pliable than we once thought.

In any case, it is more, not less important, to take exercise as you age, in order to maintain healthy joints and flexibility of movement.

So exercises, such as those in The Pop-up Gym which incorporate stability and flexibility exercises will help to keep you active and independent. They will also enable you to play sports like golf and tennis.

Taking exercise will also mean that you actually slow down the ageing process. You will look, and in all likelihood feel, younger.

'Focus on progress not perfection'.

4. I'M TOO BUSY WITH MY FAMILY

'The family that plays together stays together' is one of my mantras. Of course family commitments can put a strain on your time. However, you can adapt some of your family activities to incorporate exercise. If you have children do exercise routines with them. Create exercises that you can all do together, or have different kinds of exercise routines for each of the family that you can still engage in together. So exercise becomes a fun thing to do, not something to be avoided or squeezed in between more exciting things.

The family that plays together, stays together.

If you are thinking of exercise outside the home, remember that most leisure centres have a crèche, which means that you can enjoy a swim or join a class while your children are looked after safely.

What's best is to actually plan and design ways to be active together, so you become an active role model. Young people will pick up on subtle cues quickly, 'if you don't keep fit daddy why should I?!'

5. I'M TOO STRESSED

If you get stressed in your daily life, taking exercise is one of the most important things you can do to remedy that. It will help you in two vitally important ways. It will help you to release pent up feelings of frustration and irritability and it will replace those feelings with a mood of well-being. Secondly, the more frequently you exercise the more you will raise your tolerance of stress. So external circumstances that used to cause you stress will be less likely to do so.

6. I'M JUST TOO UNFIT TO FACE EXERCISE

When I am speaking to groups or new clients, this is often the way they have felt initially. But within a week or so of taking up exercise they changed their minds. With a little encouragement they that they were capable of more than they thought.

Don't judge yourself and your physical abilities against that of others. Many of the images that we have of fit and healthy people can seem totally out of our reach, when we first start out on the path to a more active lifestyle. We forget that fitness is attained bit by bit.

If you feel very unfit the solution is to set yourself small and reasonable targets. Notice any small improvement that you make. Just be patient and persistent. After a few weeks you will see a marked difference. You will also feel better in yourself. That will bolster your confidence to continue. By that time you will be looking forward to the exercises. They will have become part of your daily routine.

Chapter 3

Fitting exercise into your lifestyle

I have designed The Pop-up Gym to be as flexible as possible, so that it can fit into anyone's work schedule and lifestyle.

Therefore you will find that each individual exercise can be performed on its own as well as in one of the exercise routines.

One of the key attractions of this workout is that it does not require expensive gym equipment. A few of the exercises require some physical aid or prop, but these can usually be improvised using objects that you will have around you. For example, several of the exercises suggest using a backpack (see below) or briefcase instead of a dumbbell or kettlebell if you don't have one to hand. Improvise, be creative and make it fun, but couple this with common sense.

Most fitness books suggest that you carry out your exercises regularly, perhaps every other day, and at specific times. The Pop-up Gym is different. Whilst I have provided a useful initial six-week structure to the routines, I suggest that you build your exercises flexibly around your day-to-day working routines. Diarising your sessions can help you to stick to the plan, and as you will see the Pop-up promises also act to help keep you on track

Making exercise a priority

BE YOUR OWN COACH

One of the keys to enjoying movement, fitness and exercise is to give yourself 'permission' to have fun and to go for it! What do I mean by this? By using this handbook as your partner and guide I would like to invite you to 'be your own coach'. This means that you take the lead role in your health and fitness: it's time for you to be assertive; it's time for you to take control.

One of my mantras with all of my clients is that 'champions are created when no one is watching'. So, are you prepared to do the 'lonely' work that will lead to success?

What I would also suggest is that you can split up the routines of exercises if you can't fit a whole routine into just one chunk of time. However, if you do break up a routine into two time slots, make sure that you begin with a warm-up, and also cool down as you would do when working on a complete routine.

WORK THROUGH THE EXERCISE PROGRAMME STEP-BY-STEP

The exercises, once learned, take on an extra dimension when they are performed as part of a routine. The routines have been arranged in different levels of difficulty, so that each routine becomes progressively more challenging. Although many of the exercises in The Pop-up Gym look very straightforward, don't assume that they are necessarily easy to perform. Some of the techniques you will see in this book are among the most challenging that I have come across in my 15 years as a professional coach and fitness trainer. So do not underestimate how tough some of them are. There is a well-worn saying in the fitness world that 'the old ones are the best', when describing exercises and movements to their clients. Nothing could be truer of some of these moves. This is particularly

'Champions are created when no one is watching.'

true of feats of strength like The get-up (pages 108-109); 44: The single arm push up (page 115) and 46: The pistol squat (page 117). These movements are drawn from the work of the physical culturists of the later 19th century and were used as feats and tests of strength.

For that very reason, it is essential that you do not skip to a routine before you have thoroughly worked through an earlier one. It is far better to master one routine at a time and to build up your strength and experience than to dive into an advanced routine without having spent time on the earlier ones. So, for best results follow the progressions and workouts exactly as I have designed them. Do not attempt to move on to a new level until you are absolutely sure that you have mastered your current routine and that you are ready for a higher level routine.

LISTEN TO YOUR BODY

I want you to progress and achieve the best results of your life using the Pop-up Gym; however it is vital that you listen to your body and use the following guidelines to measure and assess how 'ready to train you are'. I believe 'fitness can only exist within a paradigm of health' and that you cannot truly say you are fit if you are not healthy. I have adapted the following questionairre from the work of Anderson (2002) as over many years I have found this to be a particularly quick and useful 'down and dirty' guide to overtraining, whether you are OK to train hard or if you should ease off.

Whilst there are more high tech ways to measure overtraining and readiness, in keeping with our theme, this is quick easy and validated by research.

As often as possible during the six weeks, (preferably every morning), and certainly on days where you feel extra tired or where you feel you have muscle soreness that you wouldn't expect from starting a new exercise regime, I'd like you to answer and rate the following questions:

- I slept well last night

- I am looking forward to today's workout

- I am optimistic about my future performance

- I feel vigorous and energetic

- My appetite is great

- I have little muscle soreness

Rate each of the above six statements on the following scale giving yourself the appropriate score:

1 Strongly disagree
2 Disagree
3 Neutral
4 Agree
5 Strongly agree.

If you score 20 or above then you have probably recovered enough to continue with your training. If you score below 20 then you should take a rest day or choose an easy recovery workout until your score rises again.

Eat nutrient dense, 'as-close-to-nature-as-possible' foods to build resilience

BUILDING RESILIENCE TO STRESS

More and more of the new clients I meet and talk to about their health and wellbeing cite increased pressure which affects their work-life balance. This often manifests itself as exercising less, gaining weight, sitting for longer periods of time and related illnesses. Whilst much (too much?) has been written on stress management, I'm going to take a different perspective. Whereas in the Paleolithic era we would have had a natural outlet for a physical stressor: fight or flight, modern lives have resulted in chronic mental stressors which, if left to their own devices can cause direct and indirect health problems. For more on measuring this please see Chapter 4 (page 32) on setting benchmarks and the half waist to height measurement.

THE IMPORTANCE OF RECOVERY

As well as exercising and eating nutrient dense, 'as-close-to-nature-as-possible' foods, one of the keys to building up your levels of resilience is to plan for and incorporate deliberate periods of recovery into your life. The Pop-up Gym is a six-week programme; once you have completed this I advise you to rest completely for a week before resuming. The latest research learned from military experts shows that periods of stress to the body and mind (like starting en exercise programme) require cycles of recovery to sustain long term health and resilience. In short resting and recovery allows you to improve performance long term and is great for health and wellbeing.

Here's the analogy, you are a 'whole person': this includes your 'software' (how your mind performs) and your 'operating system and power supply' (how your body performs). The key to my approach is that we use the pillars of health, exercise, healthy nutrition and restoration to build your resilience.

You are a whole person: this includes your 'software', your 'operating system' and your 'power supply'.

The result is a more focused and engaged you, if you are a CEO or business owner like so many of my clients and that of our studio, Club 51, then you will have a more engaged, more motivated from the 'inside out', happier team.

THE
ENERGY BUBBLE

Imagine that you have a bubble
of energy projecting out from your
central point and surrounding you
like a sort of science fiction force-field.
Everything stressful that happens outside
this bubble just bounces off and away from
you, leaving you calm and still inside
the bubble. So the more stressful
it is outside, the calmer you
are inside...

Now, I'm not suggesting that there really is a bubble of energy around you, but the unconscious mind doesn't distinguish between imagination and 'reality'. So if you imagine that you are shielded from stress, you will be! An extension of this idea is to use the energy bubble to help in presentations, public speaking or stressful meetings. You can extend your energy bubble all the way out to the back and side walls of the room, and then pull it in slightly to embrace and include your whole audience or fellow co-workers. The audience will notice the difference, presumably because they are unconsciously picking up the differences in your movements, facial expressions and voice tonality resulting from your imagining the energy bubble.

Chapter 4
Setting benchmarks

Before you begin the workouts, you should set some benchmarks on your current level of fitness. Whilst other fitness experts advise using complicated tests and procedures, I believe that we can get more than enough information and benchmarks from what have been called the 'Three key tests for health and longevity' based on a simple test and simple, basic human movements. Just like The Pop-up Gym workouts themselves, when designing the benchmarks I insisted that they were:

• Easy to self test

• Simple to perform

• Repeatable to measure progress.

HALF WAIST TO HEIGHT RATIO

Whilst most doctors, and experts still use the Body Mass Index (BMI) as a predictor of heart disease and diabetes, I prefer the above newer measure. Half waist to height ratio is gaining acceptance as being more predictive than BMI for what we call 'cardiometabolic' risk. Researchers on a study that analysed 300,000 people found that it was a better predictor than BMI for risk of high blood pressure, diabetes, heart attacks and strokes. Of course there are other accurate measures, but these tend to be expensive or they require going to your doctor's surgery, or a visit to another health professional. Half waist to height is easy!

Why do I prefer this test?

The body mass index does not take into account the distribution of fat around the body and as an exercise scientist I know where your body fat is stored is at least as important as how much you have. Because of its close proximity to vital organs, fat around the tummy or abdominal fat is associated with a greater risk to the heart, the liver and kidneys than is fat around the hips, bottom and extremities. Renowned stress researcher Robert Sapolsky has shown that stress actually increases your likelihood of storing fat in these areas: this is often termed 'skinny fat' by the media, but regardless of its name, it's a serious issue if you have more of it than you should.

Another thing about this test, is that I love the simplicity of its message:

'If you keep your waist circumference to less than half of your height, you will be in good shape!'

It's much easier than trying to work out and visualise your BMI.

How do you take the test? Measure your height in centimetres (or inches if you prefer). Now, simply grab a tape measure and take your waist measurement using the same units. How do you locate your waist? Take the reading mid-way between your lower rib and your iliac crest (the top of the pelvic bone at the hip). The second reading should be equal to or preferably less than half of your height.

THE ELEVATOR TEST

This test has been recently validated by Brazilian researchers and I have used different variations of it over the years. Again in keeping with The Pop-up Gym theme, it can be done anywhere and doesn't require any specific equipment. What I really like about this test is that it's really relevant and functional and has carry over to everyday life, unlike many of the gym based strength tests one sees. I see this almost as a measure of your overall longevity.

What is the test? It's the ability to sit down and rise unaided from the floor which can then predict your overall level of fitness: even completing the test using just one hand or less for support can earmark those people likely to enjoy longer lives! Why? The test is linked to physical strength, flexibility and co-ordination at a range of ages.

How do you perform the test? You have a maximum of two minutes to perform the test. Without worrying about the speed of your movement try to sit and then rise from the floor using the minimum amount of support you believe you need. Each of the two movements 'sitting' and then 'rising' is given a maximum score of five giving a composite score of ten.

One point is deducted from five for each support used (i.e. if you lean or use a hand, knee or support). A score of eight or over was linked to longer lifespan that is, use of one support on the way down and up.

Score

On the way down (out of 5) ___

On the way up (out of 5) ___

THE PLANK TEST

I use this test for all-over, total-body muscular endurance. It is based on the original work of Professor Stuart McGill. It's a 'static' test based on time to failure so have a stopwatch handy to time yourself.

1. Go down onto the floor on your hands and knees.

2. Now from lying down on your front you are going to lightly clench your fists and place your forearms on the ground under your shoulders. You're doing this test correctly when your fists are facing in opposite directions.

3. Now brace your abdominal wall and go up onto the balls of your feet so that only your feet and your forearms are touching the floor. Maintain a straight line between neck and ankles and try not to let you back bow or dip.

4. Hold this position while breathing.

How to score yourself.

The aim is to be able to to build up to two minutes for excellence.

Level 1 **Less than 1 minute** = needs more work, keep practising!

Level 2 **61 – 119 seconds** = good, keep up the good work

Level 3 **120+** = excellent

Test results

Now if you are worried about your performance on these tests, don't be! Remember the aim of the The Pop-up Gym routine is to help you improve your scores and benchmarks over time, leading to a healthier happier and leaner you. Feeling better with more zip, energy and vitality for life are great signs!

It's a great thing to know that you are motivated and on your way to achieving lasting change, whatever your specific goals. Good luck!

Other tests that may be useful

Whilst I like the simplicity of the above three tests, you can of course, also track some other measures should you wish to.

BODY WEIGHT

Scale weight can be useful, but do remember that many things can affect it, such as lean body mass, hydration status, bone density oh, and that tray of Krispy Kreme doughnuts ... these can all affect your readings! For women your weight can also vary according to where you are in your menstrual cycle. For these reasons it's important to try to standardise your reading as much as possible: use the same scales at the same time of day, wearing the same clothing (or lack thereof) and calibrate the scales using a known fixed weight to check their accuracy.

What is a healthy weight for you? Whilst there is no shortage of information around this area, there are lots of individual variances too. That's why we focus on the waist to height ratio discussed above, and look to bring overall bodyweight down to within this range. It is totally fine to measure your bodyweight and track the dial moving down along with the other measures. If you are more interested in aesthetic goals and fat loss, be sure to check out Chapter 11 on fat loss on pages 164–171.

RESTING HEART RATE (RHR)

Again, we all know that the lower the resting heart rate the better (provided you don't have an underlying medical condition causing it). The lower your RHR the more efficient your heart is at pumping oxygenated blood around your body. However, new research also shows us that RHR may actually be an independent risk factor for certain parameters of our health such as heart problems and high blood pressure. Danish researchers suggest we use the following guidelines:

Less than 50 BPM = excellent

50–90 BPM = risk gradually increases

Greater than 90 BPM = at high risk

CIRCUMFERENCE MEASUREMENTS

Taking a series of measurements around your body can be useful for tracking change and looking at problem areas with regard to weight loss. However it can be difficult to self measure with great accuracy, so this may be a better tool if you are working with a partner or a friend. Circumference measurements that can be effectively tracked are:

Hips

This measurement is taken over minimal clothing, at the widest point of the gluteal or buttock muscles. Make sure you stand erect with your weight evenly distributed on both feet and legs placed slightly apart, taking care not to tense the muscles.

Chest

This girth measurement is used to show changes in size over time of the chest and upper back region. Raise your arms to the side, place the tape meaure around the upper torso under the arms pits, then lower your arms and the measure is taken horizontally across the midline of chest after exhaling.

Upper arm

Used to demonstrate changes in the shape of the upper arm over time. Roll your sleeve up and bend the right elbow to 90°. A vertical reading is taken at the largest point. Whether you flex the muscle or not, make a note and be consistent to get accurate measurements.

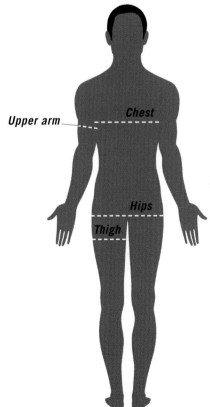

Thigh

Like the arm, this is located visually by looking for the largest point on your right leg. As this is usually quite high on the leg it may require you to roll up your shorts or trousers to identify the correct mark. The reading is taken at a 90° angle to the femur (thigh bone) which may not be horizontal.

General guidelines

SAFETY

When you are exercising think about your own safety and that of anybody else who may be around you. While you are exercising place any weights or heavy objects where you can clearly see them, so that you do not trip up on them. Similarly, when you have finished exercising do not leave weights or heavy objects lying around the floor.

When you are using a bench, chair or steps as part of an exercise ensure that it is resting on an even surface.

During my work as a Nike Master Trainer, I am involved in the education and training up of thousands of personal trainers (often at the same time). We have devised a simple system to help us and this may also help you to perform The Pop-up Gym work out safely and effectively.

The 3E's

• Proper execution: strive to use proper movements and minimise the risk of injury

• Emphasise efficiency: try to minimise wasted movements to increase control and precision

• Use expression: don't be afraid to be an 'athlete' and perform the movements with style, power, rhythm and confidence!

WARMING UP IS ESSENTIAL

Warming up and preparing for any physical activity is a must. It is really an art form in and of itself. Warming up is misunderstood and undervalued by modern gym enthusiasts, and indeed by most people who take up sports activities for pleasure.

A warm-up is an essential part of The Pop-up Gym. It elevates the body's temperature, breathing and heart rate. It has another very important function: it warms up and loosens the muscles and the joints, so it prepares your body for the exercise ahead. Going straight into an exercise without any warm-up can strain a muscle. Once the muscle is already warm, having been exposed to a warm-up, it is in much better condition to be exercised. So be sure not to skimp on this vital part of the workout.

You might find that some of the warm-up drills are more than enough to start with. That is fine. The warm-up movements in themselves are almost mini-workouts. So if you are new to physical exercise, just performing some warm-ups will be of benefit to you. Then when you are ready, maybe after a week or two, take the next step and start performing the exercises themselves.

'Think of your muscles like plasticine: when they are cold they are hard and stiff, however when you warm them up like kneading plasticine they become more pliable and ready for the tougher work ahead'

HOW HARD SHOULD YOU BE WORKING?

When you begin, you will want to familiarise yourself with the exercises and build up your strength. As you get more used to the exercises exert yourself more and start to stretch your capabilities. However, remember that the routines get progressively harder.

All of my routines use a relatively modern technique, which is to alternate high intensity, rapid exercise with low intensity, slower movements. It is known as 'interval training,' and it has won worldwide acceptance from fitness and health experts. This system not only gets great fitness results, it also burns fat faster and increases the metabolic rate to a higher level than moderate intensity training over the same period of time.

I would like you to measure how hard you are working by using a 1 to 10 scale like the one opposite. The scale is based on what fitness experts call 'the rate of perceived exertion.' So the scale is a subjective measure of how hard you are working. Basically, I would like you to work within the ranges 3 or 4 up to a 7. Beginners should make sure that they work primarily in the lower ranges, while as you become fitter and can tolerate more intensity and harder and longer training sessions, you can begin to work up to 7 and 8 for briefer periods. Again, it's easy to use and doesn't require fancy equipment!

10	I'm exhausted.
9	I'm working at my max.
8	I can't speak and I am finding this really tough.
7	I can still talk but I don't want to and I am sweating really hard.
6	I can still talk but I am slightly breathless and sweating a lot.
5	I'm fairly comfortable but I'm starting to breathe a bit harder.
4	I can carry on a conversation easily, I'm sweating slightly but am comfortable.
3	I am still comfortable, but I'm breathing a bit harder.
2	I'm comfortable and I can maintain this pace all day.
1	I'm so comfortable I could be watching TV – I barely notice this effort.

The exercises in this book have been designed to be performed in a variety of places – outdoors as well as in. So don't think that they have to be confined to a gym-like setting. Some of them are fun and amusing to do. You might even like to try them out with friends after dinner or in a park.

Many of the exercises can be combined with a walk, making your walk much more vigorous and enlivening. I really would recommend trying out some of these exercises out in the fresh air. It will add so much more to your experience of exercising.

PERSIST AND YOU WILL BE AMAZED BY YOUR RESULTS

If you follow the techniques outlined here, you will be surprised by what you manage to achieve. I would go even further. You will be amazed by the results. Within weeks you will notice some real practical benefits. This is because not only will you lose weight and become fitter, you will also develop 'functional strength'. As I explained earlier in this book, functional strength enables your whole body to perform its everyday tasks well. The exercises here involve pushing, pulling, lifting and twisting, which are just the kind of manoeuvres that your body has to make every day of your life. The Pop-up Gym will vastly improve your body's capability to carry out your daily tasks.

Having better functional strength will also mean that you will be able to play sports better or take up sports that you haven't played for a long, long time. Your joints will feel more stable, and also more supple which in turn will reduce the risk of injury, often caused by sudden movements. The exercises will also improve the stability of your body, which is another essential when playing sport.

Persist and you
will be amazed by
your results

Chapter 5
Getting and staying motivated

'Habits are first cobwebs, then cables'

Old Spanish proverb

By now you should have bought in fully to the ethos of The Pop-up Gym so you will already be making important changes, becoming more active, maybe even losing weight, or taking up a new sport or activity. So it's important to spend a little time now understanding the role of the mind and how it can influence our actions. Remember that everything you learn in this chapter goes hand in hand with the workouts and will make your results even more powerful.

1. HABITS

When learning a new skill or habit we use an area in the brain called the prefrontal neocortex, which works slowly and cautiously as it has to weigh up and makes all the complex decisions required. Once we have learned this new skill and it becomes 'second nature' or 'automacy' kicks in, the part of the brain controlling behaviour moves to an area called the basal ganglia, and we go into what is known as behavioural autopilot.

Here's an example. Imagine an elephant in the jungle looking for water. The first time it has to trample through the trees to get to the water it is really hard work and takes a long time; the process is awkward and unfamiliar. However, each subsequent time it goes back to get water, the route gets a little easier to remember until it eventually becomes a well worn pathway, 'second nature'. Habits work this way too.

So in order to change, we have to cause an interruption to 'bad' habits such as eating poorly or not exercising, even smoking, and start to engage the basal ganglia. Typically, this can be done by asking certain important questions. Recalling the previous chapter and 'Be your own coach' on page 26, take some time to answer the following ten Power Coaching questions below. These can be repeated at various points on your journey and it's

2. THE 10 POWER COACHING QUESTIONS

- What do I like about myself? What do I like about my body? What do I not like?

- What is it about my body and mind that I am unhappy with that will be positively affected by following the Pop-up Gym programme?

- What would I like to change if anything and why?

- What is my physical activity level now?

- Have I tried regular exercise before and failed to stick with it? Why is that?

- What is going on in my life that will help to faciliatate behaviour change? Or, conversely, inhibit it?

- Being realistic, how likely am I to stick with an exercise programme?

- Am I ready, really ready to try it? Would I really like to change even if it means giving up something I am accustomed to?

- Do I think that I can mobilise the mental strength and willpower to significantly change a personal behaviour if that is what I want or need to do?

- What has my previous experience of personal health behaviour change been? Good? Bad? Some success? None? What will help me this time around?

Fill these out online at **www.jondenoris.com/powercoaching** and receive the Pop-up Guide to Effective Goal Setting.

important to focus on progress not perfection. It's worth writing them out and answering in some detail to get a full picture of your state of physical and mental readiness.

Once you have answered the above you are well on the way to interrupting some of your 'bad' habits and beginning to create a new positive you.

3. FIVE POP-UP 'HABITS' YOU CAN IMPLEMENT STRAIGHT AWAY

Socialise it
Connecting with a colleague, friend or partner, or even a family member can create a social environment around your health and fitness routine; that's why it's one of my top ways to motivate yourself. The community, camaraderie and peer pressure can act as a 'check in' and keep you honest with yourself.

Diarise it
Going through the process of actually scheduling your Pop-up training session into your diary elevates it to the position of importance that it deserves. It doesn't matter what time works best for you, (I find morning suits my clients best as they have less chance of cancelling) but choose a time most likely to work for you. Evening appointments have most chance of interference as social engagements and late running meetings can act as saboteurs (see page 20).

Publicise it
Put your 'dream on the street'. What I mean by this is that by committing publicly to friends and colleagues, either in person, via email or starting your own blog about your new healthy habits you are more likely to stick with it. Once you've told people about your plans, you wouldn't want to look bad in front of them by not carrying them out or quitting early, would you?

Enjoy it

It sounds obvious, but this is vital. I meet people all the time who say they find exercise and staying active a 'chore': my experience tells me it's just a matter of time before they drop out. Apart from your Pop-up sessions, look for activities that you find fun and you are much more likely to stay on track.

Control it

Feeling like you are in control of your programme is a great way to ramp up your motivation, so I suggest you begin gradually. In exercise science we talk about becoming a 'regular exerciser'. What we mean here is that the 'regular' part is more important than the exercise part. It's fine to begin with sessions as short as ten minutes. Make sure you still incorporate the tips above. Build up to three, 10-minute sessions per week, and then you can start to add additional 10 minute blocks. Knowing you have successfully completed these Pop-up sessions, (no matter how short) has been shown to increase your likelihood of being successful further down the line – it's called 'self efficacy'.

4. WILL POWER

Sir Ranulph Fiennes is quoted as saying that if he could change one thing about himself he'd like to have 'stronger will power'. Let's just put that in perspective shall we? He's the world's 'greatest living explorer' according to the *Guinness Book of Records*; he was the first person to visit both North and South Poles by surface and to cross Antarctica on foot. Oh, and he's also summitted Mount Everest.

What is fascinating about the above statement is that actually, it should give us mere mortals hope! It should allow us to be OK, if from time to time we perceive ourselves as 'lacking willpower', the above statement should help us understand that willpower never relates to an end point, that's it's dynamic and naturally ebbs and flows. With particular reference to health and wellbeing, I like this definition:

'The conscious mental ability to follow through on plans to make change and maintain the change once it has been made.' (Jonas)

Put like this it would appear that a certain amount of willpower is not only helpful, but also necessary for us to stay on our path to wellness. It's surprising therefore that, to paraphrase author and Harvard University psychologist Dr Deirdre Barrett, 'in many circles willpower has become almost a dirty word'. Is it politically incorrect to suggest someone may be lacking willpower? If so, what do we do about it? Dr Barrett's fantastic book *Waistland* discusses this area in more detail, but we can also learn and apply some valuable lessons of our own.

Contrary to what we are normally led to believe, research tells us that willpower is trainable and can actually improve through regular practice. Whilst we know that levels of initial self control differs between individuals, we also know, more importantly that 'practising' can level the playing field (Oaten). So, in order to make the Pop-up Gym programme even more effective, we need out-smart our environment and plan for potential situations that may deplete our self-control and willpower.

The work of Howard Rankin and others has also highlighted a useful analogy, that of treating 'willpower' just like any other muscle that needs to be 'flexed' regularly in order to improve. Just like with exercise, I insert a note of caution. In the same way as if you take on too much physical exercise, too quickly, overdoing initial attempts to exert self-control can lead to setbacks. Whilst researching for my Masters degree in the area of behaviour change theories, I quickly learned that

'Gradual change leads to permanent change'.

And this has now become a key mantra of The Pop-up Gym. Whilst it is great to get quick reductions in body fat, increased fitness and energy levels, most fitness plans will promise this. What's unique about The Pop-up Gym is that the techniques below will help empower you to control your health and fitness forever. Here are some exercises you can do to exercise your willpower muscles.

Visualisation
This technique has long been used by eastern European sports scientists. You can think of it a bit like running a 'home movie' in your mind of you being successful at a certain future behaviour. For an Olympian, that behaviour could be mentally rehearsing running at world record

pace or height, however for us it might be something as simple as seeing ourselves walking past the local sweetshop without going in, or lacing up our trainers before going out for a jog.

Sit in a comfortable place, with your legs and arms uncrossed. After assuming a relaxed position close your eyes and recall a time when you achieved your best, this might be getting to the gym in which you excelled or did your absolute best. For example this might be when you ran a great 5K race, it can be anything that was meaningful to you. Try to visualise the scene as vividly as possible.

Eight questions to help you visualise

1. Where were you? Indoors or out?

2. What time of day was it?

3. What was the weather like?

4. What could you see? What could you hear?

5. Picture yourself immediately beforehand: what were you wearing?

6. What were the physical sensations you could feel?

7. What were you thinking about at the time?

8. What were your emotional feelings at that time?

The images that you create during visualisation must be as vivid, detailed and accurate as possible as you actually send subtle nervous impulses to your muscles whilst you are doing this. Soviet researchers called this 'ideomotor training' with reference to elite sport, but we apply it here to flexing our 'willpower' muscle and visualising times when we were in our own state of 'flow' and positive about our ability to improve our own health and fitness in the future.

'Near misses'

Whilst keeping yourself out of harm's way can sometimes be helpful, for example, manipulating your environment by taking a different route home to avoid the temptation of a burger and fries, an alternative is to

practice what I call 'near misses' or 'desensitisation'. First perform your
visualisation: let's say it was around walking past the local bakery,
where you would typically cave in and buy a doughnut. The aim is to
gradually expose yourself to the tempting situation, so first begin by
walking past and just looking in the window. It takes practice so try it a
few times. Next, you would go into the bakery and take a look at all the
items on display (it maybe helpful to have a coach or friend come with
you). Keep practising until you can eventually sit in the bakery, perhaps
having a coffee, without the need for the cakes. People who are successful
at this technique report an enormous sense of empowerment as they
regain control. Try this with any food which you feel can be tempting to
you. After practising the 'near misses' you can safely move on to ...

'Bite size'
This requires a little experimentation, and is the ultimate flexing of
your will power muscles! Here you are going to test yourself to see if it's
possible for you to have just one bite of a burger, one biscuit and not the
whole pack, one sip of beer ... can you then set it down and walk away?
If so, it can be useful to know that this food doesn't actually hold any
'control' over you. If you can't resist, then you have already learned two
techniques that will help you to avoid these foods instead.

When you successfully resist temptation
you are developing self-control.

At this point you may be asking, 'yes, but what happens when things go wrong and I have a setback?'

It's a good question and it's important to plan for while expecting that you will have set backs along the way. We don't like them, but we need a way to deal with them, a plan or a strategy. Peter Gollwitzer, a Professor of Psychology at New York University specialising in goal setting and planning coined the term 'action trigger'. We can use these action triggers to create 'instant habits' or what we will call 'Pop-up promises'.

I want you to create your first Pop-up promise right now, then, once you have successfully implemented it, you should add one more Pop-up promise every week thoughout the six-week programme.

These promises will be similar to IF THEN statements, but they are specifically centred around proactive health and fitness related habits that you want to achieve consistently.

POP-UP PROMISES

Examples
IF 'I miss a day at the gym'
THEN 'I will go the next day before work'

IF 'I have carbs for breakfast'
THEN 'I wont have any for lunch or dinner'

The Pop-up promises need to be written down so that you can go back and check in on them, remember them and use them particularly when you feel like you are in danger of slipping up. Use the promises to help improve your self talk, (that internal civil war that you have with yourself each time you are faced with either going for a run or meeting friends for a drink.) I really encourage positive self talk and have a strict rule with all my clients at Club 51: 'No negative self talk'. Some clients automatically go into negative self talk patterns, but whatever the reason, it's never a good habit and it can really influence everything from body language, posture, energy levels and the way you think. Lastly, own your promises, keep them specific, but simple, so that you can remember them and action them, starting now.

Your weekly promises

Week 1	If:	
	Then:	
Week 2	If:	
	Then:	
Week 3	If:	
	Then:	
Week 4	If:	
	Then:	
Week 5	If:	
	Then:	
Week 6	If:	
	Then:	

Chapter 6
Getting and staying supple

Introduction

In this chapter I am going to show you some great techniques to help you to maintain supple joints and overall mobility. These techniques can be applied at home, in a gym, park or office, in fact anywhere! They use little or minimal equipment so there are no excuses! You may even find that this part of the book helps you to resolve issues with pain, prevent injury and, in conjunction with the main programme improve athletic performance.

Our current lifestyle has become dependent on modern technology, and although this has made our life easier, we are also more sedentary. With more hours spent sitting than ever before, there is a greater threat to our overall mobility and postural balance. Therefore, keeping your joints supple as shown in this chapter, can be very restorative and helpful.

To perform any given movement in our body we need good joint stability as well as joint mobility. Joint stability refers to the ability to maintain or control joint movements or positions. Stability is achieved by the coordinating actions of surrounding tissues (ligaments, muscles capsule) and the neuromuscular system. Conversely, joint mobility is defined as the degree to which an articulation (where two bones meet) is allowed to move before being restricted by surrounding tissues (ligaments, tendons, muscles).

A lack of joint stability will affect the joint's mobility leading to dysfunction and possible injury. This is often attributed to a lack of joint control due to certain muscles becoming inhibited and others becoming tight. The illustration below will help you to understand this balance. The relationship between stability and mobility is analogous to a 'see saw' with the body at its best when they are balanced.

Different types of stretches

TO STRETCH OR NOT TOO STRETCH?

In recent times, there has been a fair amount of controversy around the subject of flexibility and stretching. While research has shown that static stretching is quite effective in improving range of motion, it has also been demonstrated that it can reduce force and strength (as it inhibits the muscles being stretched). My advice is that this type of stretching is best done at the end of any training session or, as a distinct session in its own right, but not before strength training or Pop-up Gym sessions.

Before training and during the warm-up is a great time to use what we call 'dynamic stretching' as it has a better effect on muscular performance: dynamic stretching drills can be found within the main programme sections on page 66. In summary, the major health and fitness organisations recommend regular flexibility work to maintain supple joints, and my favourite go-to techniques are below.

STATIC STRETCHING

This is one of the easiest flexibility techniques you can use. It consists of lengthening a muscle or muscle group by slowly moving a joint into its available range of motion and then holding that position for a set time, I usually suggest 15 to 30 seconds. There are many studies supporting the use of static stretching as part of an exercise routine to improve muscle pliability. I like to view muscles like plasticine: when you warm them up they become springy, but when cold, they are brittle and more likely to snap. Static stretching should be mainly used after training.

ACTIVE STRETCHING

Active stretching is when you 'actively' contract your muscles when they are in the stretched position rather than using an external force, as above in static stretching. It is ideal as part of a warm-up as it not only improves flexibility but keeps muscles strong while going through the available range of motion. This type of stretching allows you to exceed the static range of motion as encountered during exercise and sport.

DYNAMIC STRETCHING

Actively taking the body's joints through their full available range of motion whilst applying gradually increasing force and energy can be defined as dynamic stretching.

This is my favourite type of movement to include in a pre-activity warm-up, and the various movements such as leg swings, skipping and various drills can become an exercise routine in their own right and when done properly are quite demanding. You need a good level of core stability and balance prior to undertaking a dynamic stretching programme, and performing it will make you even stronger. I suggest using dynamic stretching exercises, for one set of ten to fifteen repetitions per movement in a controlled way.

FASCIAL RELEASE

'Fascial release' refers to a series of techniques used to reduce restrictions in movement caused by a tissue called fascia. Fascia is basically a tissue that covers all of our muscles: think of it as being a bit like a spider's web. Sometimes it can tighten and create adherences in and between muscles and limit their movement.

There are various ways to use fascial release, and it can be easily applied either with your own hands or by using a foam roller, a golf ball or tennis ball for example. With your thumbs or golf ball, you apply pressure to the muscle/area and slide or roll it along the muscle slowly thereby releasing it. Don't forget to pause and hold for 30 seconds on tender spots as they are indicative of fascial restriction/adherence around a muscle

TRIGGER POINTS

Trigger points are areas of regional pain that may affect one or more muscles or groups of muscles. A trigger point is often defined as a hyperirritable spot, usually found within a taut band of muscle or in the muscle fascia. When you compress or push down on a trigger point it can feel uncomfortable and can give rise to referred pain to other areas. Trigger points are a common cause of pain and can lead to dysfunction in the muscular system.

It is intimately related with fascial pain and therefore can be treated using the same method. Use your thumbs to apply compression to reduce the painful area or use a golf ball or fascial tool to try and get the same effect depending on the area of the body. They key to this technique is that you must sustain the pressure until you feel the pain or discomfort begin to fade which is usually after about 30 seconds or so.

10 ways to stay supple

1. STEP AND TWIST

This position (often used in yoga) targets lots of muscles along the back and legs.

Starting on all fours, straighten the legs and raise the hips. From here move your left foot forward between your hands. Keep your left palm flat

to the floor. Slowly raise your right arm straight up to the ceiling. Try and twist from the spine, rib cage and waist, not by throwing the arm back.

Keep your hips levelled and twist a little deeper as you breathe out.

Hold the position for 5 to 10 seconds and then switch arms. Repeat 5 times on each side. Avoid overreaching.

2. CHILD'S POSE

Another position with origins in eastern movement techniques; it can be very helpful to help you maintain mobility in your lower back. Start by kneeling with both knees on the ground, sit back on your heels. (You want your feet to be pointed so the tops of your feet are completely touching the ground.) Lean your torso over your thighs, and straighten your arms overhead resting your forehead on the floor. Hold the position for about 10 seconds and repeat 10 times.

3. HAMSTRINGS

As you can see from the photos, there are two ways of performing this stretch.

On the first you start by lying down on your back. Keep your left leg bent and your foot on the floor. Wrap a towel around the foot of your right leg and slowly start rising up with the knee straight. Once you start feeling the stretch behind your thigh, hold that position for 30 seconds. Change for the other side.

An alternative would be to the stretch in an active way: in this case you would be lying down on your back, but this time you would raise your leg using the contraction of the muscles on the front of your thigh to move it further. Repeat five times and hold each contraction for five seconds and rest for five seconds between each repetition.

To perform the second version, you should keep one leg straight, bend one knee slightly and then slowly start leaning your torso down with your back straight. You will know when you need to stop as you will feel the hamstrings stretching, but not allowing your torso to go further.

Again, hold the position for 30 seconds.

Version 1

1

2

Version 2

4. LOWER LIMBS/CALVES

Start by placing your hand on the wall and gradually move your feet away from it. Slide your right foot back and slowly start leaning forward making sure you have good body alignment, i.e. shoulder, hips and ankle in a straight line. Hold the position for 30 seconds once you start feeling the stretch on your calves.

5. PLANTAR FASCIA RELEASE USING A TENNIS/GOLF BALL

Stand on the tennis ball and slowly roll the sole of your foot over it. Each time you find a painful spot, stay there for about 30 seconds or just long enough to feel the pain coming down. Breathe deeply while you are doing this. Roll the ball through the whole sole backwards and forwards and sideways. Repeat daily, even several times a day, and especially after exercising. To get a deeper effect, use a smaller, harder golf ball. This technique is fantastic for alleviating tightness in the ankle, calf, knee and even the hip areas. Clients who play sport, (particularly football) find much relief from this technique

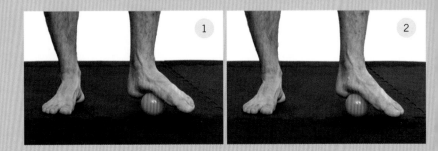

6. BUTT AND GLUTEAL FASCIAL RELEASE USING A TENNIS BALL

Sit down on the floor, bend your legs and place your left foot on the top of your right knee. Place a tennis ball under your left glute and tilt a little bit to the left, toward the outside. Roll around slowly until you find a tender spot. Stay on it while breathing deeply until the pain goes away.

7. PECTORAL FASCIAL RELEASE USING A TENNIS BALL OR GOLF BALL

This technique is particularly good for helping improve posture, it relieves tension in tight necks, shoulders and chest area. It can be done using either a doorway, or from the floor. If you try this from the floor be sure to you're your elbow and place your arm behind your back as this helps get the body in the right position to really feel the release. Search for tight spots in the area around the chest muscle and shoulder muscle and roll the ball into these areas releasing the tight fascia around the muscles. Perform a couple of times on the tight area.

8. IT BAND FASCIAL RELEASE USING A GRID ROLLER

Lie down on your right side and place the grid foam roller under your right hip. Put as much body weight onto it as you can tolerate and begin searching for the dreaded trigger points. Roll on top of the grid roller until it reaches the knee and back again towards the hip. Stay on the tender spots until the pain decreases. You can use a tennis ball or various other tools that are harder/softer to your own personal preference.

9. PIRIFORMIS/BUTT STRETCH

Lie on your back with your legs extended and your back straight. Keep your hips level and your lower back down on the floor. Bend your left knee, placing the left foot flat on the floor. Cross your right ankle at your left knee. Grab the back of your left thigh and clench your fingers around it. Slowly bring it towards your chest. Breathe deeply for 30 seconds. Repeat on opposite side.

10. MEDICINE BALL CHOP AND LIFT

This dynamic stretch will help you warm-up for your workout at the same time as it improves mobility on the hips, spine and shoulders.

Grab a medicine ball and stand with your feet shoulder-width apart.

Keeping your arms straight, bring the ball to the outside of your right hip and perform a squat. Push down and out with your feet (into the ground) and 'chop' the medicine ball diagonally across your body so that as you stand up, your legs are straight and the ball is now above your left shoulder.

Keep your core braced and make sure not to round your lower back.

Repeat 10 times and then switch to the other side.

Chapter 7

The exercises: 55 ways to total fitness

This is one of the most important exercises in the whole series of routines. It underpins all the other movements that you will do.

Tighten your abdominal muscles as if you were expecting someone to punch you in the stomach. Hold the position for a few seconds. Your back may feel firmer as a result. This is because your abdominals and your back muscles support each other. If you strengthen your abdominal muscles efectively you are less likely to suffer from back problems in your everyday life.

CORE

1. Abdominal bracing

key to the exercises

These exercises underpin the entire Pop-up Gym programme. Most of them work the whole body but others concentrate on building strength in specific areas. The figure on each exercise indicates the part of the body that is the focus of that exercise.

2. Internal hip rotation

This move can form part of a warm-up drill before you start a routine. It can also be used as an exercise in its own right. This exercise loosens up the whole body. It moves the hips, the torso, the legs and arms.

Performing this movement is a bit like walking and dancing at the same time. The body becomes very fluid. From a standing position, start to walk, and as you do flick your left heel out to your side to touch your hand, keeping your knee in a central position. Then do the same exercise with your right leg.

How you flick the heel is important. Look at the picture: the leg is slightly flared, it is not at a straight angle. By kicking in this way you rotate the hips which is one of the purposes of this movement.

WARM UP /
COOL DOWN

3. Backpack clean

This looks deceptively easy to perform but is a tough exercise to execute correctly. It involves a number of key stages and is a total body exercise. To carry out this exercise you can use a backpack (as in the images below) or a holdall. If you have access to a gym of course this can be performed with a bar or a powerbag.

1 Begin by bracing your abs and keeping your back in neutral.

2 Lower down into the bottom of a squat position. Extend your hips and knees simultaneously as you pull the bag upwards from the floor. There should be no change in spinal position as you pull upwards. As the pack passes your knees, scoop your hips forward, (a triple extension: hips, knees and ankles) keeping the pack as close to your body as possible.

3 Pull yourself under the weight so you are in parallel front squat position.

4 Drive upwards and press the pack above the head.

5 Control the bag or bar on the bring down to return to the start position with the arms bag close to chest.

DYNAMIC / WHOLE BODY

4. Bent over row

Pop-up Gym

The bent over row exercise also uses a bag or briefcase. Its primary aim is to strengthen the back and the legs. It will also strengthen the arms and much of the upper body.

Begin by bracing the abdominal muscles and keep the back in neutral position. Lower the body from the hips, with the hips at about 45 degrees, allow a slight bend at the knee and lower the bag to just below the knees. Then, while maintaining that bent over position, raise the bag to your chest and slowly lower back with resistance to start position.

UPPER
BODY
·
LOWER
BODY
·
CORE

The bodyweight squat mainly strengthens the legs, and to a lesser extent it also works the buttocks and the abdominals.

Starting from a standing position with your legs shoulder width apart, maintain a tight core and neutral back and lower yourself down into a squat. Push your buttocks out; your back will go into a slight curve (neutral) which is meant to happen. As you lower yourself put your arms straight out in front with your hands touching each other.

Now raise yourself back up into a standing position and lower your arms.

To carry out this exercise properly you need to ensure that your hips and knees are in alignment. A common mistake is to allow the knees to drift inwards/outwards. You will see in the picture that the ankle, knee and hips are all aligned with each other.

intermediate

When you raise yourself back up into a standing position put your hands behind your head. Then lower yourself down again into a squat keeping your hands behind your head. This is a slightly tougher exercise than the first one. It uses the upper body a little more, opening out the chest and the thoracic spine. It's a good exercise for strengthening your posture.

advanced

As with the pictures below, do the squat whilst holding a bag or a weight if in the gym, to add more load.

LOWER
BODY

6. Boxing

Now for four boxing movements. These will strengthen the core of your body as well as giving your arms a work-out. You can carry these out as shadow boxing or by using light hand weights.

The first punch is a jab. Putting your left leg forward, you push out your left arm straight in front of you, while your right hand is raised to protect the side of your face (2)

The second punch is called a cross. In this movement you rotate your body and throw your arm straight at your opponent. In the boxing world this move is often called a one, two, because the first punch with the left or right hand is followed by the second punch from the other hand.

The photo shows a right cross (3) with your left leg forward and your abdominals nice and tight, throw your right arm straight ahead. At the same time you are protecting the left side of your face swivelling the body as you do so. Repeat this movement with your left arm punching ahead and covering the right side of your face with your right arm.

The third punch is a hook. Keep your core nice and tight, your elbow bent, and with a bended arm punch across your opponent rather than straight at him. Again, protect the other side of your face. So this is more of a rounded movement with a much shorter punch than in the jab or the cross. The photo shows a left hook (4)

The fourth punch is the upper cut. (5) Here you are punching upwards. Hold your core tight, turn the hips slightly inwards as you punch with the glove palm facing back towards you. Make sure that your other arm is covering the unprotected side of your face. Try the move with a left and then right upper cut.

DYNAMIC
/ WHOLE
BODY

advanced

Work with a partner and use hook and jab pads.

7. Burpees

This is a tough series of movements. It exercises the whole body and it moves the body up and down, which is why it taxes the muscles and uses up a fair bit of energy. It will get your heart going, and if you do this quickly you will find that your breathing quickens.

So, if you're doing this exercise for the first time, you will probably want to do it slowly. Later, you can speed it up, so that it becomes a more dynamic movement.

DYNAMIC / WHOLE BODY

beginner

Rather than driving back with both legs simply step back one leg at a time into the high bridge, and then step forward one leg at a time, back through to standing.

1 ......▶

2 ......▶

5 ......▶

6 ......▶

Start in a standing position, with your feet at about shoulder width apart with your hands by your side. Keep your core firm. Bend down and reach for the floor in a crouching position as in photos 2, 3 and 4. Your knees should be under your chest and your glutes turned on and tight. Drive both feet back into a high bridge position (photo 5) and then back up so they are under the chest. Finally, come back up to a standing position.

3 ············▷   4 ············▷

7 ············▷   8

LOWER
BODY

8. Chain gang

Pop-up Gym

This exercise is good for strengthening the gluteals, that is, the buttock muscles. You will need a light band to give your muscles some resistance. You can use a belt or a strap. In the picture you will see that a resistance band is being used.

Tie the band around the feet. Ensure that your core is firm and take short steps forwards, backwards and sideways holding the band. As you move you will be pushing against the resistance band, which will work your gluteals and lower back quite intensively.

You may find this exercise a bit difficult at first because you probably don't use your gluteal muscles very much. Most people tend to have underdeveloped gluteal muscles. Weak gluteal muscles can result in back problems. What this exercise does is to train you to use your leg and buttock muscles when lifting, so that they are sharing with the back the work of lifting.

This exercise is the opposite of the internal hip rotation move on page 68 as, instead of moving the legs outwards to touch your hands, they move inwards.

Kick your left leg inwards to your right side and touch your left heel with your right hand. Then do the same movement with your right leg.

Remember to keep your body straight as you see in the picture, maintaining a firm core and neutral back.

This exercise is good for strengthening your legs, your back and your core. It will also improve your posture.

WARM UP / COOL DOWN

10. Dan John's goblet squat

This is another all-round exercise. It is a variation on the squat. Ideally, you should perform it with a kettle bell as in the picture, but you could substitute that with some other small heavy object.

Get yourself in a standing position, brace your abdominal wall and keep a neutral back. Grasp the object with both hands holding it just below the chin, making sure that your palms are facing inwards, then lower your body till your elbows are resting on your knees, with the object still held below your chin.

Now move your body from side to side, still holding the object in place. Then return to a standing position.

This exercise works a lot of muscles. You want to be working all your muscles evenly, not putting a strain on any of them, so be aware of what you are doing, especially around your abdominal muscles and back.

LOWER
BODY

This is an excellent exercise for the hamstrings (the muscles behind the upper leg), the buttocks and the calves. It also works the hips and the extensor muscles. This exercise is sometimes called a flutter kick.

The aim of this exercise is to bring up your heels alternately to touch your buttocks. Remember to keep a strong posture throughout the exercise. You can carry it out while walking up and down a room, or while you're out walking or jogging.

1

2

LOWER
BODY
·
WARM UP /
COOL DOWN

12. High knee drill

This exercise complements Heel to butt on page 79. The beginner level for the exercise is to start by walking. As you get fitter, can increase the pace.

Start in a standing position with your hands stretched out in front of you just above your waist. Raise your knees alternately to touch your hands, alternatively you can adopt a sprinters' posture as the in the photo.

This may prove a difficult exercise for you, as it is with most adults. However, young children are usually able to perform this exercise quite naturally. It is a movement that most of us stop doing as we grow up, which is a pity as it not only strengthens the leg and buttock muscles, but also the lower back.

Persistence will bring its rewards. If you continue trying to do this exercise you will eventually master it. You might surprise yourself.

LOWER
BODY
.
WARM UP /
COOL DOWN

13. Hip aeroplane

This exercise is the brainchild of a Canadian back and spinal rehabilitation specialist, Professor Stuart McGill. He taught it to me and showed me its unique value. It rotates the hips and improves the body's balance and rotational force.

Standing with a nice, clean, straight posture, your stomach muscles slightly taut, put your left leg forward and your right leg well back. Hinge forward as in the picture (1) as if you were being an aeroplane, with your arms out as you might have done as a child.

Now, the trick is to rotate your whole body upwards to your right so you are rotating anti clockwise, keeping your arms straight and your back straight also, the body is fairly rigid encouraging whole body stability. Then repeat the movement on the other side changing legs.

LOWER
BODY
·
CORE
·
WARM UP /
COOL DOWN

14. Jumping Jack

This is a great exercise for warming up the body and preparing it for some serious exercise. This exercise in itself will work all your muscles.

Standing straight with your abdominals tight, your back firm but neutral and your ankles tight, raise your arms above your head. Let your arms touch and then move them slightly apart. Then lower your arms and as you do kick both feet out and then bring them back together again. This is quite a dynamic exercise. It will raise your heart beat, make you sweat a little and may make you out of breath for a few moments afterwards.

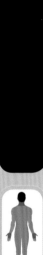

DYNAMIC
/ WHOLE
BODY
.
WARM UP /
COOL DOWN

This exercise works all the core muscles and many others as well. Like the Jumping jack it will get your heart rate up.

Standing firm and straight, legs slightly more than shoulder width apart, hold a bar or stick above your head. (In the picture you see an 8 kilo bar, but you can use something simple like a broomstick). Then lower yourself to the floor, still holding the bar above your head, ending up kneeling on one knee and then on both knees. Then move back to standing position.

LOWER
BODY

16. Lateral lunge

This exercise uses all your muscles especially your lower body and core.

Start this exercise from a standing position with your trunk muscles held firmly in place and engaged. Step your left leg out to the side creating a large lunge position, bending the left leg at the knee and keeping your right leg straight. Lower your body and touch your left foot with both hands. Remember to keep your back upright and head up. Using your core and gluteal muscles raise yourself up to standing position again. Repeat stepping out to the right.

LOWER
BODY

information

In exercising, as in life, movement occurs in a combination of three directions or 'planes'. These are known as:

Sagittal: movement that is back and forth (front to back)

Frontal or lateral: sideways movement

Transverse: a movement that swivels or rotates part of the body

Pop-up Gym uses balanced movement across all three planes.

17. Rotational step-up

This movement is a variation on the conventional step-up. It uses all the muscles of the lower body, i.e., the calves, ankle muscles, thighs, the glutes, the hamstrings and the quads. The quads are the four muscles that form the front of the thigh.

Start by standing beside a bench, tighten your core and hold your hands just touching the edge of your hips. Place your right leg onto the bench so that there is a 90 degree angle between your feet. Then move your body round towards the bench and place your other foot upon it. You will then have rotated your hip 90 degrees as you stood fully on the bench.

Move back into your original position, reversing the stages and moving one leg at a time, then practise the same movement beginning with your left leg facing the other way.

LOWER
BODY

Pop-up Gym

This exercise strengthens the leg , knee and ankle muscles. In doing so it tests your balancing power.

Use a skipping rope or any other long rope, but do not raise the rope over your head like skipping. It 's not that kind of exercise.

Holding the rope in both hands in front of you, tighten your abdominal muscles and stand on one leg, then hop over the rope. When you have completed that movement the rope will be behind your legs. Next hop back over the rope. You then repeat those two movements with your other leg.

LOWER
BODY
·
WARM UP /
COOL DOWN

This can also be done with a stick.

19. March on the spot

This movement is similar to the Internal and External hip rotation exercises in that it moves the entire body very dynamically. Like those two exercises it will get your heart rate up.

Starting from a standing position, hold your core tight and your back in neutral, and raise your legs, so that your knees are roughly at right angles to your body. (You can do this exercise while walking or just standing on the spot.) Keep your knees high and your elbows high too. Notice that in the picture the arms and legs are nicely aligned. It is a good exercise for improving your posture.

This exercise has many uses. It is not only an exercise in itself, it can also serve as a Warm-up exercise. I often use the march as an active recovery between exercises or as part of a warm-up drill, or in between circuits.

WARM UP /
COOL DOWN

20. Medicine ball straight chop

CORE
·
DYNAMIC
/ WHOLE
BODY

Pop-up Gym

This is another exercise that really works the trunk, but it also strengthens the arms and the thighs. To do this exercise properly it is absolutely essential that you begin with a correct posture. So once again, maintain a neutral back and keep your abdominals tight.

Start by standing with a medicine ball in your hands, and raise the ball directly above your head, as if you might be about to chop a piece of wood with an axe. Then bring down the ball, and as you do so lower your body into a squat position, so that the ball ends up between your legs at a height just above your ankles. Then come back up into your starting position.

beginners

Keep palms pressed together throughout to create tension (no ball).

advanced

Add weights or a pause-hold for 2 seconds at the bottom position.

21. Medicine ball wood chop

This exercise is based on the same concept as the last one, but with two differences. With this exercise you start near the ground in a squat position, and you then move your body up diagonally, rather than in a straight line.

So get into the squat position, tighten your core and keep your back in neutral, and hold the ball out towards your right as in the picture. Then swing the ball high up towards your left. At the end of this movement the ball will be raised above your head.

beginners	advanced
Keep palms pressed together throughout to create tension (no ball).	Add weights or a pause-hold for 2 seconds at the bottom position.

CORE
·
DYNAMIC
/ WHOLE
BODY

22. The pop-up

This is quite a dynamic exercise as it will work most of your muscles and it will move your body through several levels: you will stand, crouch, lie with half your body on the floor, move your body from your waist and then you will rise up again to a standing position. So your body will be moving quite dynamically, and your heart rate will increase.

Begin by holding your body as in the first picture, firm but not stiff, with your legs slightly bent, and your arms raised at the elbow with your hands facing outwards. Then move down into a crouching position, touching the floor with your hands and resting the balls of your feet on the floor. Then, while keeping your hands on the floor, move your legs back behind you, with only the balls of your feet touching the floor, and then move your body up as far as you can from the waist. Then return to the starting position.

DYNAMIC
/ WHOLE
BODY

23. Power skip

Pop-up Gym

This movement is like a skip but you do it with a lot of power, hence the name, 'power skip.' You can do this on the spot or while out walking. Just skip along, but really work those arms and legs, driving through the air athletically with your arms and with your knees bent high. The more vigorously you do this exercise the greater its impact upon you. Have some fun with this exercise, and enjoy the essence of this as children do. It is such a joyful movement.

DYNAMIC
/ WHOLE
BODY

This is quite a fast exercise.

Stand on the balls of your feet and keep stiff through the ankles and knees. The movement is a short staccato type rhythm.

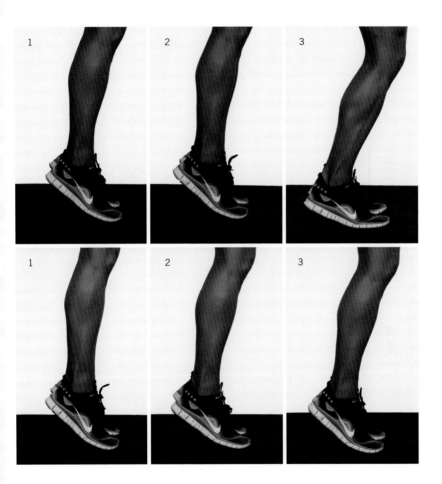

LOWER
BODY

25. Single leg dead lift balance

This exercise strengthens the core and the muscles of the upper and lower back. It also tests your powers of balance. For this exercise you will need a small object such as a backpack like the one in the photo.

Start from a standing position holding your abdominal wall tight and begin to hinge towards the backpack with your right leg on the ground and your left leg raised up to waist height (photo 2). As you hinge reach forward to touch the pack with your left hand keeping the back in neutral. At the same time allow the left leg to reach backwards hovering off the ground. Then repeat the movement with your right arm touching the backpack and right leg reaching backwards.

LOWER
BODY

advanced

Use a lower object, but maintain a neutral back position.

This is a dynamic drill for stretching and working a range of muscle groups including the hamstrings and the hips. This is another exercise where it is essential to hold the core firmly in place, and not to allow it to sag.

This exercise uses arm movements that are similar to those in the march, but the legs kick up in a straight line, and then swing back.

LOWER
BODY

WARM UP /
COOL DOWN

Pop-up Gym

This exercise is good for working the leg and trunk muscles. It also strengthens posture, improves balance and agility.

Start by standing next to a flat bench, tighten your core, place your hands by your sides, and then step up onto the bench with the left leg and then the right. Try keeping the body straight as in the picture. Make sure that you do not slouch, and stay focused. Repeat on the other side.

beginner	advanced
Use a lower step.	Add additional load.

LOWER
BODY .

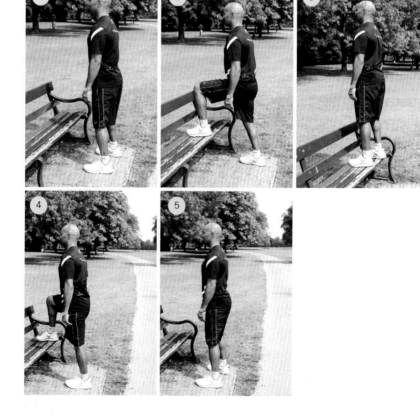

28. Anterior or front lunge

This exercise uses all the muscles of the lower body.

Stand straight with your core braced and your hands out to the sides as in the photo. While keeping a straight back, take a long, deep step out with your right leg whilst lowering your body; your right knee should end up just off the ground, foot placed firmly on the floor. There should be an approximate 90° angle at both knees. Now, drive yourself back from this position, returning to standing. Repeat this exercise, using your left leg. This is an intermediate exercise.

advanced

Use dumbbells or a medicine ball to add more resistance.

1

2

3

4

5

LOWER
BODY

29. Triple punch with dumbbell

This exercise uses a nice, light dumbbell, of about 3 to 5 kilos. This exercise will obviously work your arms and strengthen your back and torso, but the main aim of it is to increase the heart rate. There is no need to use a heavier weight. This exercise is about stamina not strength.

Standing with a dumbbell in each hand make small punches up towards the ceiling and down again, alternating your left and right arm.

Then from the same position extend the arms outwards, again alternating from left to right, as in the picture.

Then in the third position, while keeping a neutral back, bend at the hips and with a sight bend at the knees punch with the weights straight down until you have fully extended one arm and then the other but without locking the joints.

DYNAMIC
/ WHOLE
BODY

1

2

30. Mid-range rotation with medicine ball

This is a great exercise for the core and upper body.

From a standing position, hold a light medicine ball at chest level, slightly lean from the hips, maintaining a neutral back, bend the knees slightly, and keep the ball locked onto the body, with your elbows out at the side. Then rotate your trunk to the left and then to the right. The chest and the ball should be moving together. You are therefore rotating the trunk. You are not moving it sideways, you are just rotating it, as in the picture.

advanced

Do the exercise very fast.

CORE

31. Bodyweight kneeling push-up

This exercise works the upper body, that is, the chest, the arms and shoulders. It also works the core.

Begin with your knees on the floor, holding your abdominals tight. Your body should form a straight line from the shoulders to the hips. Your hands should be resting underneath your shoulders. Lower your body on to the floor and then lift yourself up in a straight line keeping your knees on the floor.

UPPER
BODY
·
CORE

32. Beginner push-up to row

Pop-up Gym

This exercise is a variation on the push-up. It strongly works the core, and also the arms and legs. It can be performed in a variety of ways: with dumbbells as in the picture or without them.

Begin this exercise as you would with a traditional push-up, making sure that your abdominals are tight and your back is in neutral. When you are at the top of the push-up, i.e., when your body is fully raised, lift the left arm off the floor, supporting your whole body with your other arm, and return it to the ground now repeat on the right arm.

DYNAMIC
/ WHOLE
BODY

advanced

Perform the exercise using a dumbbell.

33. The bridge or plank

This is quite a tough exercise, but it sure is worth doing because it strengthens the core and the lower back: those all-important pivotal parts of the body.

Lie on the floor supporting yourself on your folded arms and on the balls of your feet, exactly as you see in the picture. Then, having tightened your abdominals and keeping your back in neutral, lift your body off the floor until it is in a plank-like position. Remember to keep the balls of your feet on the floor. Hold that position for up to 2 minutes, maintaining the body in a nice straight line.

Once you are proficient, you can add another dimension to the exercise. It is a tougher, more advanced version. Instead of resting on your folded arms, rest on your hands, but still have the balls of your feet on the floor. Once you have raised your body into the plank position, move your hips and lift one leg off the floor, and then the other. So this exercise works your hips and your gluteals even more than the first one.

advanced

Perform alternating on single leg, which is much tougher on the core and glutes.

CORE

34. Bottoms up shoulder press

FEAT OF STRENGTH

UPPER
BODY

This exercise uses a kettlebell, but you could use a dumbbell instead, or a small hand-weight or even a can of beans! This exercise works the shoulders and also the lower back. Using a kettlebell makes this exercise tougher than if you use a dumbbell or any other weighted object, because the kettlebell's weight sits vertically above the hand grip. So when you use the kettlebell you have the added task of having to balance the weight.

Stand with your legs shoulder width apart. Hold the weight in one hand near your head, while holding your other arm outstretched at right angles to your body. Then lift the weight away to the side of your head, while moving your other arm at a 45 degree angle. Then stretch out your arm that holds the weight, so that your upper arm is at right angles to your body and your forearm is pointing directly at the ceiling. Finally, raise your weighted arm to its full length with the weight almost above your head and your other arm pointing downwards to the floor. Then repeat with your other arm.

1

2

35. Chin-up / pull-up

One of the toughest exercises to do, this exercise tests the upper body, primarily the back and arms, it's also great for your core. If you don't have your own chinning bar, you can use a door frame and hang from the top of the frame itself (very tough!) or you can buy a bar that will fit a door frame.

Starting with your abdominals braced, hang from the bar with your palms facing outwards, almost try to 'bend the bar' as you grip creating tension. Begin to raise yourself upwards to the bar, so that you finish the move with your chin just above. Then lower yourself back to the starting position.

Alternate grip

FEAT OF
STRENGTH

UPPER
BODY
.
CORE

beginner

This exercise becomes a little easier if you hang with your palms facing inwards because you can get some more assistance from your arms.

36. Core push-up

This is a push-up with a difference. Instead of moving your body up and down to the floor as if it were a plank, when you drop to the floor with this version you bring one knee up to touch your elbow. This exercise gives you shoulder and core stability, as well as strengthening your arms, shoulders and abdominals.

So holding your core tight, get into the position that you would if you were performing the standard push-up. As you lower your body, bring your left knee forward to touch your left elbow, then straighten your left leg, as you push back up. Now repeat on the other side, bringing up your right knee to touch your right elbow.

UPPER
BODY
·
DYNAMIC
/ WHOLE
BODY

37. Crawl

This is another exercise that develops the core muscles. It is a very demanding one; it entails crawling forwards and backwards. You can also practise it crawling sideways.

Get down on the floor on all fours, holding your core tight, move your right arm forward and your left leg forward also. Then move your left arm forward and your right leg forward. Remember that throughout this exercise only your hands and the balls of your feet should be on the floor. The rest of your body will be above the floor.

DYNAMIC
/ WHOLE
BODY

38. Kettlebell get up

FEAT OF
STRENGTH

CORE
·
DYNAMIC
/ WHOLE
BODY

Pop-up Gym

In this demonstration, a shoe is used to teach the movement, focusing on balance and technique. Later you can progress to using a kettlebell if you have one, a dumbbell or light handweight.

Lie on your back with a shoe placed on top of your clenched right fist. Keep your elbow tucked in and your thumb pointing towards your head. Allow your shoulder to drop back into its socket and wind up your left arm to create a stable position. Keep your eyes focused on the shoe/kettlebell.

Bend the right knee, and keep the right foot flat on the ground. Keeping your right arm straight, actively drive up through your right leg and come up onto your left elbow and forearm. The goal is to keep your elbow and shoulder in line and your trunk braced (see abdominal bracing)

Sit up and plant your left hand on the ground, ideally with your hand aligned with your shoulder; think about getting the armpit forward. Keeping the glutes squeezed push off the ground using your right foot and extend your hips.

Supporting the weight of your body with your left arm and right leg, pull your left leg underneath your hips and plant your knee underneath your centre of mass and in alignment with the shoe/kettlebell.

Still keep your eyes locked on the shoe, get your trunk vertical. Now, push off your right leg and drive upwards to the standing position. Use your left arm as a counter balance if you need to.

Once standing, it is important to remember that you are only mid way through the movement! To complete the 'get up', you should unwind and reverse the sequence to return to the floor exactly as you got up.

beginner	advanced
Use a shoe or other light object.	**Increase weight of kettlebell used.**

38. Bodyweight hip raises

This exercise works all the muscles around the lower back, the hips, the hamstrings and calves (extensor chain). You can do this exercise using a bench, the edge of a staircase or with a chair.

From a position lying down on your back, place your heels on the chair, keeping your body nice and straight, your core tight and your palms flat on the floor. Then raise your hips, holding them high so that your body is held in an extended position. Now lower your body gently back to the ground.

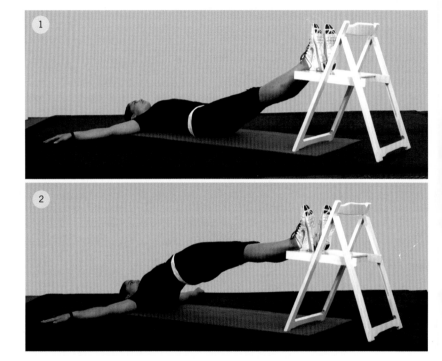

CORE
.
LOWER
BODY

advanced

Perform the exercise using just one leg.

39. Push up

The push up is one of the classics of fitness training and no programme based around bodyweight exercise would be complete without it and some variations of it.

The push up is great for the upper body and abs, and many other muscles of the body. Begin in the high bridge position and place your hands under your shoulders. Now make sure your elbows are pointing back towards your feet and 'screw' your hands into the ground to activate your back muscles and create that all-important tension. It's almost as if you were trying to bend a bar between your hands. Now using your breathing and not allowing your back to drop or sag, lower yourself down under control and drive back up to the top position.

UPPER
BODY
·
CORE

40. Medicine ball push-up

Pop-up Gym

This exercise is a variation on the normal push-up; it works the triceps and chest and is also designed to activate the core musculature. Feet should be shoulder width apart and hands are placed on the medicine ball so you have a narrow grip. Once you are in position lower yourself towards the floor and then come back up again, keeping your core tight throughout this movement.

UPPER
BODY
·
CORE

This is a variation on the medicine ball push-up. You keep only one hand on the medicine ball, with the medicine ball right underneath the shoulder. You need to maintain a really tight core. As you lower and raise your body you will be working that shoulder much more than in the original medicine ball push-up.

UPPER
BODY
·
CORE

43. Mountain climber

This exercise is similar to the burpee. Begin as if you were going to start a push-up or burpee, with both hands firmly on the floor and the balls of your feet touching the floor. Then bring forward your left leg to touch your elbow and then do the same with your right leg. Continue this exercise alternating your left and right leg.

CORE
·
DYNAMIC
/ WHOLE
BODY

beginners

Hover the foot off the ground for
more core focus.

advanced

Make the movement dynamic, fast
alternating left and right legs.

This is another advanced exercise. It is very tough and very intense. It uses the whole body. The best progression for this move is to begin with the hand elevated on a small box or bench, but in our diagram we are showing the full version of this difficult move, expertly demonstrated by my fellow comrade Jamie Stumpe.

- Place feet slightly wider than shoulder width apart, facing down.
- Brace your abdominal wall (see bracing prep drill on p67).
- Spread your fingers apart for balance with most of your weight under your heel of palm under the little finger.
- Pull yourself down wards with your lat / back muscle.
- Visualise 'screwing' the hand into the ground as you drive downwards and upwards.
- Keep maximal tension in the entire body using power breathing.
- Eliminate all soft spots, keep tight.

FEAT OF STRENGTH

UPPER BODY
·
DYNAMIC / WHOLE BODY

45. Beginner pistol squat

The beginner pistol squat variations are slightly easier. The exercise is the same as in the pistol squat except, that you trail one leg behind you, not in front. That gives you much more balance and puts less pressure on the leg that is supporting you. Other variations are squatting to a box to reduce range of motion), and beginning by lowering with both legs and performing the 'concentric' phase (coming up) as a pistol (single leg). Use a partner to assist you.

LOWER
BODY
.
DYNAMIC
/ WHOLE
BODY

46. Pistol squat

This is one of the toughest exercises. It works the legs, the buttocks and the lower back, and it will test your stability. It is called a pistol squat because when it is done well it looks like a pistol. It is almost impossible to perform this exercise without a little curve in your back.

Do not attempt this exercise if you have knee problems, because it will be too demanding, it's tough enough and that's why I have put it in the feats of strength – a circus trick!

Begin with a light weight either a kettlebell or dumbbell held in your hands. This actually helps make the move easier as it acts as a counter balance. Extend your left leg straight out in front of you, and slowly lower yourself down on one leg, keep the chest up, the back straight (it will round out a little at the bottom) and the shin as vertical as possible throughout.

The pistol is all about tension, so power back up out of the bottom position.

key teaching points

Grip the floor with the foot, reach forward ensuring your glutes and hamstrings are working.

Think about pulling yourself down slowly with the hip flexors.

Visualise punching through the ground with your heel as you stand up.

Drive your hips forward and power breathe.

Don't let your knee slide forward or bow inwards.

FEAT OF STRENGTH

LOWER BODY

DYNAMIC / WHOL BODY

47. Split jump

This is another quite demanding exercise. Put very simply you jump up and down, landing alternately on your left foot and then your right. It develops the strength and power of your lower body and is often used as a plyometric exercise (very quick). Start with your left knee bent forward at 90°, your core nice and tight, your right leg trailing behind you, your right elbow up with your hand held high, jump up and switch leg positions, landing on your right foot, with the right knee bent forward.

LOWER
BODY
.
DYNAMIC
/ WHOLE
BODY

48. Squat jump

This is an advanced version of the squat. It is an excellent all-round exercise that really works the body and gets your heart rate up. Yes, it is difficult, but that is part of its attraction. It will give you great satisfaction when you have completed it.

So begin as you would with a normal squat, you can use a medicine ball or some lightweight object if you want to (advanced). However, initially you could practise this exercise just using your own weight and then progress from there.

Lower your body into the squat position, then jump up into the air stretching your arms high above your head into extension. As you come down again into the squat position, remember to be soft on the knees and try use the lower body muscles to act as shock absorbers.

LOWER
BODY
·
DYNAMIC
/ WHOLE
BODY

49. Swiss ball 'stir the pot'

This is another excellent exercise for the core. In this exercise you are only moving your forearms on a swiss ball, also known as stability ball, I've adapted this from renowned spinal rehab professor Dr Stu McGill.

Begin with your forearms resting on the ball, and with the balls of your feet on the floor. Keep your abdominals tight and your body in a nice straight line, stretching all the way from your ankles, through your hips up to your shoulders. Now, make small circles on the ball with your forearms. Your arms are moving on the ball, which puts pressure on your core to stabilise itself. You might think that your core will be doing nothing, but in fact it will be doing quite a lot.

CORE

50. Band pull

This exercise is primarily for strengthening the back and arms, and is also great for improving posture. Begin with a light resistance band (one you can do 15 repetitions with comfortably) and attach securely to a door or a tree. The band should be in line with your chest and your arms should be outstretched in front of you (1).

Now, ensuring your palms are facing each other, pull the band towards you, finishing with your elbows bent and hands almost under your armpits (2). You should feel the muscles in your back contracting at this point, pause and return to the starting position.

UPPER
BODY

This exercise works almost all your muscles. It is great for building up your core and for strengthening your whole body stability.

Begin as you would with a normal bridge, and then start to lift your right arm off the floor keeping the elbow bent at 90 degrees, you finish having rotated the body 90 degrees. Then lower the body back into the bridge position and repeat with your left arm.

51. Side plank rotation

beginner

Hold up for 60 seconds.

advanced

Combine with dynamic movements or repetitions to either side.

FEAT OF STRENGTH

CORE
·
DYNAMIC
/ WHOLE
BODY

52. Walk out

Pop-up Gym

This is a deceptively demanding move as it requires you to change level and also works the whole body, it can be used as an all-round fitness test and also as a preparatory move for more complicated exercises.

Start from a standing position holding your brace your core with your back in neutral. Then lower your body and begin to walk out one arm at a time until you reach the top of the bridge or push up position. But do remember to keep your abdominals tight otherwise you will put too much pressure on your lower back. From this position you pause and then reverse the movement walking backwards with your arms and finishing in the standing position.

Creative options include combining the walk out with push ups, mountain climbers, superman drills and others to create challenging mini routines to test yourself with.

CORE
·
DYNAMIC
/ WHOLE
BODY

53. Superman

Get into position by lying on your front on the floor. Now lift one arm off the floor and the opposite leg off the floor, (for example raise your left arm off the floor and your right leg. Hold your body totally still, come down to the floor, then change sides.

intermediate	advanced
Perform from kneeling position.	This move can be done as part of your walk-out movement sequence from the high bridge position.

Intermediate

CORE
·
DYNAMIC
/ WHOLE
BODY

54. Grave diggers

Also known as shovelling and a close cousin of the wood chop exercise (page 89). In this move you pivot through your hips, performing a shovelling movement, this exercise can be done quickly to generate a metabolic effect, using a diagonal movement pattern challenges the entire trunk especially the obliques and lower back muscles.

CORE
·
DYNAMIC
/ WHOLE
BODY

55. Kettle bell swings

This is one of the few exercises in the Pop-up Gym routine where you need some kit, a kettle bell. The exercise can also be performed with a light dumbell if you can't get hold of a kettle bell. What is the swing?

Here we use one of the most underused exercise techniques, the hip hinge to perform the swing. When done correctly it's one of my favourite moves and fantastic for all round body strength and power. It has great transfer to sport and also helps keep your back healthy.

Begin by grabbing the kettle bell, now begin to swing the kettle bell, by hinging through your hips, with minimal knee bend. At the bottom of the swing keep the kettle bell close to the groin, and at the top of the movement the kettle bell should go no higher than shoulder height, with absolutely no leaning back past vertical (a common mistake). Visualise a wall behind you so you can't lean back; your back should stay in neutral throughout.

CORE

DYNAMIC / WHOLE BODY

Chapter 8

Warm up, cool down

THE IMPORTANCE OF A WARM UP

The aim of any warm-up is to prepare the body for the tougher work ahead, it's a vital part of any workout regime and I've gone one stage further in our programme by creating a strategic Warm-up which will increase body temperature and heart rate, make your muscles more pliable and begin to focus your mind. It will also improve what we call 'bio-motor skills' that have a transfer to everyday life by improving posture, the way your body moves and increasing functional flexibility.

Those of you who are totally new to movement and exercise and are unsure if you are ready for the Pop-up Gym workouts should begin by attempting to complete Warm-up drills 1 and 2 (overleaf) twice through (comfortably) before attempting the Pop-up Gym workouts. These should be combined with the preparatory exercises in this chapter and the movements from Chapter 6.

COOLING DOWN

Just as we needed to gradually prepare the body for tough exercise through the warm-up phase of the workout, it also makes sense to gradually reduce the intensity of the session, allowing the various systems of the body to return to normal. This helps you to unwind from the training session, letting the heart rate and blood pressure get back to normal. Evidence that a cool-down prevents muscle soreness is mixed and a certain amount of mild delayed onset muscle soreness (DOMS) is to be expected when beginning a new exercise programme, or increasing the intensity or duration of a programme. Performing some light cardio work, cycling, walking or jogging whilst gradually reducing the intensity for three to four minutes should be sufficient to remove waste products and cool down.

Warming up and cooling down are like using the gears in your car. You don't go from neutral straight to fifth, and you don't screech to a halt every time you stop.

Warm up drills

WARM-UP DRILL 1

1. MARCHING ON THE SPOT – 30 secs

2. LIGHT JOGGING ON THE SPOT – 60 secs

3. HIGH KNEE DRILL – p.80 60 secs

4. HEEL TO BUTT DRILL – p.79 60 secs

5. MEDICINE BALL STRAIGHT CHOP – p.88 30 secs each side

6. HIGH KNEE DRILL – p.80 60 secs

7. HEEL TO BUTT DRILL – p.79 60 secs

8. BODYWEIGHT HIP RAISES – p.110 x10

WARM-UP DRILL 2

1. MARCHING ON THE SPOT
30 secs

**2. LIGHT JOGGING/
SKIPPING** 60 secs

**3. EXTERNAL HIP
ROTATION – p.77** 60 secs
(alternate legs)

**4. INTERNAL HEEL
ROTATION – p.68**
60 secs (alternate legs)

**5. LIGHT JOGGING/
SKIPPING** 60 secs

**6. EXTERNAL HIP
ROTATION – p.77**
60 secs (alternate legs)

**7. INTERNAL HEEL
ROTATION – p.68**
60 secs (alternate legs)

8. WALK OUTS – p.122 x 8

WARM-UP DRILL 3: ALTERNATIVES

1. SKIPPING 6–7 minutes

2. RUNNING 6–7 minutes

3. CYCLING 6–7 minutes

As an alternative, you can perform 6-7 minutes of skipping, cycling, or light walk-running for your Warm-up.

PREPARATORY EXERCISES

Preparatory exercises are general movement patterns or techniques complex exercises later on.

Abdominal bracing (right)

Tighten your abdominal muscles as if you were expecting someone to punch you in the stomach. Hold the position for a few secs. Your back may feel firmer as a result. This is because your abdominals and your back muscles support each other. If you strengthen your abdominal muscles you are less likely to suffer from back problems in your everyday life.

The chain gang (lateral step with resistance band) (below)

You will need a light band to give your muscles some resistance. You can use a belt or a strap. In the picture you will see that a resistance strap is being used.

Tie the band around the feet. Ensure that your core is firm. Then take short steps forwards, backwards and sideways holding the band. As you move you will be pushing against the resistance band, which will work your gluteals quite intensively.

Crawl patterns

Fantastic for building all round strength and functional mobility, crawl patterns can be added into Warm-ups or done when you have some open space, they are quite liberating especially when you use multi directional crawling: definitely one to grab attention!

Bird-dog

Get into a bridge position, and lift one arm off the floor and the opposite leg, e.g., raise your left arm off the floor and your right leg. Hold your body totally still, come down to the floor, then change sides.

Chapter 9
The workouts

Now you have seen each of the individual moves from **The Pop-up Gym** it's time to put them together to create your very own programme. This is where the magic happens! I have created a programme which combines the two most effective training methods I have used with my clients: **interval training** and **high intensity training.**

Interval training is a technique that involves alternating periods of intense effort and low to moderate effort. Interval training boosts metabolism significantly longer than a steady training session of longer duration, it helps build lean muscle faster than steady exercise and burns more calories than a steady intensity workout.

With **high intensity training** the aim is to safely achieve muscle fatigue through maximum efforts and quick bursts coupled with recovery. It takes advantage of the afterburn effect, increasing oxygen demands and burning calories.

Combining these two techniques maximises fat burning and lean muscle building in a significantly shorter time. These routines require dedication and determination, but if you have got this far through The Pop-up Gym you are ready for the challenge!

Although you don't need any fancy equipment to do The Pop-up Gym workouts, you might find that some small items will help make the workouts more productive:

• A hand towel, water bottle and stopwatch.

- Light dumbbells, medicine balls of different weights, kettle bells and a fitness ball could all be helpful too.

The main programme is six weeks in duration, and each individual session has been designed to achieve specific fitness goals. These sessions are highlighted in red and you will achieve the best results when you follow the whole plan, in its exact format.

However I also have plenty of options for you to adapt it to your own unique needs and lifestyle. For example follow the Quick fix workouts (short intense workouts designed for when you don't have too much time or are on the move, traveling on business). I also have **beginners** and **advanced** options for those of you who find the programme needs adjusting to your current levels.

You will also find supplementary sessions placed strategically through out the weekly progressions, marked in green. These sessions are interval based sessions which are more cardiovascular in nature, they compliment the actual work out days themselves. On these days I would like you to choose a more aerobic based activity such as cycling, walking, running, skipping or swimming as your exercise alternative.

DAY 1 BENCHMARKS

The first day of the The Pop-up Gym challenge, be sure to take the tests from the benchmarks chapter. There's a form on page 173.

PERFORM WARM-UP DRILL 1 (PAGE 128) 5 MINUTES.

Workout

Perform each number group twice before moving on to next number.
So perform 1A, 1B, 1C then go back and repeat, then move on to 2A
and so on.

1A. BODY WEIGHT SQUATS **1B. BODYWEIGHT HIP** **1C. MARCHING/JOGGING**
– p.71 10 reps | **RAISES – p.110** 10 reps | **ON SPOT – p.87** 1 min

PERFORM TWICE

2A. BENT OVER ROWS – **2B. BODYWEIGHT** **1C. MARCHING/ JOGGING**
p.70 10 reps | **KNEELING PUSH-UPS –** | **ON SPOT – p.87** 1 min
| **p.101** 10 reps |

PERFORM TWICE

3A. BRIDGE OR PLANK – **3B. SUPERMAN – p.123** **1C. MARCHING/ JOGGING**
p.103 30 seconds | 10 reps each side | **ON SPOT – p.87** 1 min

PERFORM TWICE

Cool down

Pop-up Gym

PERFORM WARM-UP DRILL 2 (PAGE 129)

Workout

Perform each number group twice through before moving on to the next. For example perform 1A, 1B, 1C, go back and repeat, then go on to 2A.

1A. STEP UPS – p.96
10 reps

1B. BEGINNER PUSH-UP TO ROW – p.102 10 reps

1C. MARCHING/ JOGGING ON SPOT p.87 1 min

PERFORM TWICE

2A. LATERAL LUNGE – p.84 10 reps each leg

2B. POWER SKIPS – p.92
20 reps each leg

1C MARCHING/ JOGGING ON SPOT – p.87 1 min

PERFORM TWICE

3A. HIP AEROPLANE – p.81 10 each side

3B. SWISS BALL STIR THE POT – p.120
30 seconds then change direction

1C. MARCHING/ JOGGING ON SPOT – p.87 1 min

PERFORM TWICE

Cool down

DAY 5

Five on five off

Choose your exercise mode: cycling, running or another cardio exercise. Warm-up at a lower intensity for 5 minutes (RPE 3/4) and when you feel you are fully warmed up, we are ready for the main block of exercise. Perform 5 minutes of higher intensity exercise, at an RPE of 6 or 7. Now perform 5 minutes of lower intensity exercise at an RPE of 4/5. Repeat this sequence two more times and then perform a cool down at a lower intensity again (RPE 2/3) for 5 minutes. Total work time = 40 minutes

DAY 6

Follow Chapter 6 Getting and staying supple as your workout today.

DAY 7 IS A REST DAY IN WEEK 1

Week 2

Workout days 1 and 3

PERFORM WARM-UP DRILL 1 (PAGE 128)

Workout

1A. MEDICINE BALL STRAIGHT CHOP– p.88
15 reps

1B. DAN JOHN'S GOBLET SQUATS – p.78 15 reps

1C. MOUNTAIN CLIMBERs – p.114 1 minute

.... **PERFORM TWICE** ....

2A. MEDICINE BALL WOOD CHOP – p.89
15 reps each side

2B. FULL PUSH-UPS – p.111 10 reps

2C. MOUNTAIN CLIMBERS – p.114 1 minute

.... **PERFORM TWICE** ....

3A. SINGLE LEG DEAD LIFT BALANCE – p.94
10 reps each leg

3B. SIDE PLANK ROTATIONS – p.121
10 rotations/reps

3C. MOUNTAIN CLIMBERS – p.114 1 minute

.... **PERFORM TWICE** ....

Cool down

PERFORM WARM-UP DRILL 2 (PAGE 129)

Workout

1A. BODYWEIGHT SQUATS – p.71 10 reps

1B. BODYWEIGHT HIP RAISES – p.110 10 reps

1C. MARCHING/JOGGING ON SPOT – p.87 1 minute

········· PERFORM TWICE ·········

2A. BENT OVER ROWS – p.70 10 reps

2B. BODYWEIGHT KNEELING PUSH-UPS – p.101 10 reps

2C. MARCHING/JOGGING ON SPOT – p.87 1 minute

········· PERFORM TWICE ·········

3A. BRIDGE OR PLANK – p.103 30 seconds

3B. SUPERMAN – p.123 10 reps each side

2C. MARCHING/JOGGING ON SPOT – P.87 1 minute

········· PERFORM TWICE ·········

Cool down

Week 2

Workout days 4 and 6

PERFORM WARM-UP DRILL 1 (PAGE 128)

Workout

1A. STEP UPS – p.96
10 reps

1B. BEGINNER PUSH-UP TO ROW – p.102 10 reps

1C. JUMPING JACKS – p.82
1 minute

 **PERFORM TWICE**

2A. LATERAL LUNGE – p.84
10 reps each leg

2B. POWER SKIPS – p.92
20 reps each leg

1C. JUMPING JACKS – p.82
1 minute

PERFORM TWICE

3A. HIP AEROPLANE – p.81
10 each side

3B. SWISS BALL STIR THE POT – p.120 30 seconds
(then change direction)

1C. JUMPING JACKS – p.82
1 minute

PERFORM TWICE

Cool down

DAY 5

Five on five off

Choose your exercise mode, cycling, running etc. Warm-up at a lower intensity for 5 minutes (RPE 3/4) and when you feel you are fully warmed up, you are ready for the main block of exercise. Perform 5 minutes of higher intensity exercise, at an RPE of 6 or 7. Now perform 5 minutes of lower intensity exercise at an RPE of 4/5. Repeat this sequence two more times and then perform a cool down at a lower intensity again (RPE 2-3) for 5 minutes. Total work time = 40 minutes

DAY 6 IS A REST DAY IN WEEK 1

DAY 7

Follow Chapter 6 Getting and staying supple as your workout today

PERFORM WARM-UP DRILL 1 (PAGE 128)

Workout

1A. BACKPACK CLEANS
(use dumbbell, kettle bell
or other weight) – p.69
15 reps

1B. BODY WEIGHT SQUATS
– p.71 15 reps

1C. HEEL TO BUTT KICKS –
p.79 1 min

PERFORM 3 TIMES

2A. BURPEES – p.74
15 reps

2B. FULL PUSH-UPS –
p.111 10 reps

2C. HIGH KNEE DRILL –
p.80 1 min

PERFORM 3 TIMES

3A. ANTERIOR LUNGE –
p.97 10 reps each leg

**3B. BODYWEIGHT HIP
RAISES (single leg) –**
p.110 10 reps each leg

3C. POWER SKIPS – p.92
1 min

PERFORM 3 TIMES

Cool down

PERFORM WARM-UP DRILL 2 (PAGE 129)

Workout

1A. STEP UPS – p.96
15 reps

1B. BEGINNER PUSH-UP TO ROW – p.102 15 reps

1C. JUMPING JACKS – p.82
1 min

······· **PERFORM 3 TIMES** ·······

2A. LATERAL LUNGE – p.84 12 reps each leg

2B. POWER SKIPS – p.92
20 reps each leg

1C. JUMPING JACKS – p.82
1 min

······· **PERFORM 3 TIMES** ·······

3A. HIP AEROPLANE – p.81
10 each side

3B. SWISS BALL STIR THE POT – p.120
30 seconds (then change direction)

1C. JUMPING JACKS – p.82
1 min

······· **PERFORM 3 TIMES** ·······

Cool down

Week 3

Workout days 2, 5 and 7

DAY 2
Five on five off

Choose your exercise mode, cycling, running etc. Warm-up at a lower intensity for 5 minutes (RPE 3/4) and when you feel you are fully warmed up, we are ready for the main block of exercise.

Perform 5 minutes of higher intensity exercise, at an RPE of 6 or 7. Now perform 5 minutes of lower intensity exercise at an RPE of 4/5. Repeat this sequence two more times and then perform a cool down at a lower intensity again (RPE 2/3) for 5 minutes. Total work time = 40 minutes.

DAY 5
Beat me back

Choose your form of exercise, let's say you choose walking or running. Now, pick a route and walk or run out for 20 minutes (actually time it). Now, turn back, follow the same route your goal for this session is to try and beat the time it took you to go out. Of course, the terrain will differ depending where you are but that doesn't matter, the beauty of this session is that it's the increase in intensity towards the latter half of the session that's important.

DAY 7
3:1

Follow the drills in the warm-up for 5 minutes. This session is interval based again but with shorter more intense work periods and longer relative rest times. Choose your exercise from the cardio based options, lets say skipping or running. You are going to skip for 3 minutes at an RPE of 3/4 (comfortable pace) immediately alternate this with 1 minute of hard skipping or running (harder pace RPE 7).

Repeat this block four more times for five rounds of 4 minutes at a ratio of 3 low intensity, 1 higher intensity hence 3:1!

PERFORM WARM-UP DRILL 2 (PAGE 129)

Workout

1A. MEDICINE BALL STRAIGHT CHOP – p.88 20 reps

1B. MEDICINE BALL NARROW PUSH-UPS – p.112 15 reps

1C. BODYWEIGHT SQUATS – p.71 20 reps

1D. BENT OVER ROWS – p.70 20 reps

1E. ANTERIOR LUNGES – p.97 10 reps each leg

1F. POWER SKIPS – p.92 20 reps each leg

············· **GATHER YOURSELF AND REPEAT 3 TIMES** ·············

2A. BURPEES – p.74 15 reps

2B. CORE PUSH-UPS – p.106 12 reps

2C. MOUNTAIN CLIMBERS – p.114 20 reps

2D. BAND PULLS – p.120 20 reps

2E. SQUAT JUMPS – p.119 15 reps

3F. MID-RANGE ROTATION WITH MEDICINE BALL – p.100 20 reps

············· **GATHER YOURSELF AND REPEAT 3 TIMES** ·············

Cool down

Week 4

Workout days 2, 5 and 7

DAY 2

Beat me back

Choose your form of exercise, let's say you choose walking or running. Now, pick a route and walk / run out for 20 minutes (actually time it). Now, turn back, follow the same route your goal for this session is to try and beat the time it took you to go out. Of course, the terrain will differ depending where you are but that doesn't matter, the beauty of this session is that it's the increase in intensity towards the latter half of the session that's important.

Now, perform the fascial release and stretches from the Suppleness chapter.

DAY 5

This is an alternative type of session designed to challenge your fitness in a slightly different way. Although I have suggested cycling, you can also use running, skipping, or even walking depending on your individual level, remember the undulating intervals are vital to this workout.

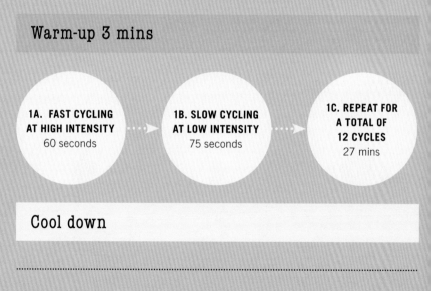

Warm-up 3 mins

1A. FAST CYCLING AT HIGH INTENSITY
60 seconds

1B. SLOW CYCLING AT LOW INTENSITY
75 seconds

1C. REPEAT FOR A TOTAL OF 12 CYCLES
27 mins

Cool down

DAY 7

Follow Chapter 6 Getting and staying supple as your workout today.

You will need a kettle bell or dumbbell for this session. Whilst this session may look deceptively simple, it is very tough to perform through from start to finish. Using a stop watch, you are going to work for 15 x 1 minute blocks.

Warm-up drill (below)

JUMPING JACKS – p.82 1 minute

POP-UPS – p.90 10 reps

.... **PERFORM 3 TIMES** ....

Workout

1A. KETTLE BELL SWINGS – p.125
(beginners use an 8kg, intermediates
a 12kg and advanced a 16kg)
20 seconds

1B. PUSH-UPS – p.111 6 reps

REST TILL THE TOP OF THE MINUTE

Repeat for 15 rounds of one minute. Start swinging again at the top of every minute. Make harder by increasing swing time or number of push-ups.

Week 5

Workout days 1 and 3

PERFORM WARM-UP DRILL 1 (PAGE 128) OR 3 (PAGE 130)

Workout

1A. ROTATIONAL STEP UPS – p.85 15 reps

1B. BEGINNER PUSH-UP TO ROW – p.102 15 reps

1C. JUMPING JACKS – p.82 1 minute

····················· **PERFORM 3 TIMES** ·····················

2A. LATERAL LUNGE – p.84 12 reps each leg

2B. POWER SKIPS – p.92 20 reps each leg

1C. JUMPING JACKS – p.82 1 minute

····················· **PERFORM 3 TIMES** ·····················

3A. HIP AEROPLANE – p.81 10 each side

3B. SWISS BALL STIR THE POT – p.120 30 seconds (then change direction)

1C. JUMPING JACKS – p.82 1 minute

····················· **PERFORM 3 TIMES** ·····················

Cool down

PERFORM WARM-UP DRILL 2 (PAGE 129)

Workout

1A. BACKPACK CLEANS
(use dumbbell, kettle bell
or other weight) – p.69
15 reps

1B. BODYWEIGHT SQUATS
– **p.71** 15 reps

1C. HEEL TO BUTT KICKS –
p.79 1 min

PERFORM 3 TIMES

2A. BURPEES – p.74
15 reps

2B. PUSH-UPS – p.111
10 reps

2C. HIGH KNEE DRILL –
p.80 1 min

PERFORM 3 TIMES

3A. ANTERIOR LUNGE –
p. 97 10 reps each leg

**3B. BODYWEIGHT HIP
RAISES SINGLE LEG –**
p.110 10 reps each leg

3C. POWER SKIPS – p.92
1 min

PERFORM 3 TIMES

Cool down

Workout days 2, 5 and 7

DAY 2
Five on five off

Choose your exercise mode, cycling, running etc. Warm-up at a lower intensity for 5 minutes (RPE 3/4) and when you feel you are fully warmed up, we are ready for the main block of exercise. Perform 5 minutes of higher intensity exercise, at an RPE of 6 or 7. Now perform 5 minutes of lower intensity exercise at an RPE of 4/5. Repeat this sequence two more times and then perform a cool down at a lower intensity again (RPE 2/3) for 5 minutes. Total work time = 40 minutes

DAY 5
3:1

Follow the drills in the warm-up for 5 minutes. This session is interval based again but with shorter more intense work periods and longer relative rest times. Choose your exercise from the cardio based options, let's say skipping or running. You are going to skip for 3 minutes at an RPE of 3/4 (comfortable pace) immediately alternate this with 1 minute of hard skipping or running (harder pace RPE 7). Repeat this block four more times for five rounds of 4 minutes at a ratio of 3, low intensity 1, higher intensity, hence 3:1.

DAY 7

An alternative session today. I would like you to do between 60-90 minutes of cardio exercise preferably outside. This should be done at a pace where you can still talk, between 5-6 on our RPE scale (rating of perceived exertion). If you are feeling energetic then this is the perfect session to use a weighted jacket or backpack (see Chapter 11 for fat loss strategies).

You will need a kettle bell or dumbbell for this session. Whilst this session may look deceptively simple, it is very tough to perform from start to finish. Using a stop watch, you are going to work for 15 x 1 minute blocks.

Warm-up drill (below)

JUMPING JACKS – p.82 1 minute

POP-UPS – p.90 10 reps

PERFORM 3 TIMES

Workout (in 1-minute blocks)

1A. KETTLE BELL SWINGS – p.125
(beginners use an 8kg, intermediates a 12kg and advanced a 16kg)
30 seconds

1B. PUSH-UPS – p.111 6 reps

REST TILL THE TOP OF THE MINUTE

Repeat for 15 rounds, each round is one minute start swinging again at the top of every minute. Make this session harder by increasing the weight of the kettle bell or performing 20 rounds (20 minutes)

Week 6

Workout days 2 and 4

PERFORM WARM-UP DRILL 2 (PAGE 129)

Workout

1A. MEDICINE BALL WOOD CHOP – p.89
20 reps

1B. MEDICINE BALL NARROW PUSH-UPS – p.112 15 reps

1C. BODYWEIGHT SQUATS – p.71 20 reps

1D. BENT OVER ROWS – p.70 20 reps

1E. ANTERIOR LUNGES – p.97 10 reps each leg

1F. POWER SKIPS – p.92
20 reps each leg

·········· **GATHER YOURSELF AND REPEAT 3 TIMES** ··········

2A. BURPEES – p.74
15 reps

2B. CORE PUSH-UPS – p.106 12 reps

2C. MOUNTAIN CLIMBERS – p.114 20 reps

2D. BAND PULLS – P.120
20 reps

2E. SQUAT JUMPS – p.119
15 reps

3F. MID-RANGE ROTATION WITH MEDICINE BALL – p.100 20 reps

·········· **GATHER YOURSELF AND REPEAT 3 TIMES** ··········

Cool down

DAY 3

This is an alternative type of session designed to challenge your fitness in a slightly different way. Although I have suggested cycling, you can also use running, skipping, or even walking depending on your individual level, remember the undulating intervals are vital to this workout.

Warm-up 3 minutes

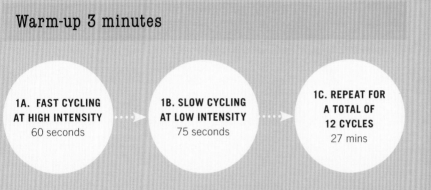

1A. FAST CYCLING AT HIGH INTENSITY
60 seconds

1B. SLOW CYCLING AT LOW INTENSITY
75 seconds

1C. REPEAT FOR A TOTAL OF 12 CYCLES
27 mins

Now, perform the fascial release and stretches from Chapter 6 Getting and staying supple (pages 62–63).

DAY 5
Five on, five off

Choose your exercise mode, cycling, running. Warm-up at a lower intensity for 5 minutes (RPE 3/4) and when you feel you are fully warmed up, you are ready for the main block of exercise. Perform 5 minutes of higher intensity exercise, at an RPE of 6 or 7. Now perform 5 minutes of lower intensity exercise at an RPE of 4/5. Repeat this sequence two more times and then perform a cool down at a lower intensity again (RPE 2/3) for 5 minutes. Total work time = 40 minutes

DAY 6

Follow Chapter 6 Getting and staying supple as your workout today.

Week 6

Workout day 7

PERFORM WARM-UP DRILL 1 (PAGE 128) OR 3 (PAGE 130)

JUMPING JACKS – p.82 1 minute

POP-UPS – p.90 10 reps

.... **PERFORM 3 TIMES** ....

Workout

 →  →

1. KETTLE BELL SWINGS – p.125 10 reps

2. DAN JOHN'S GOBLET SQUATS – p.78 10 reps

3. PUSH-UPS – p.111 10 reps

 →  →

1. KETTLE BELL SWINGS – p.125 9 reps

2. DAN JOHN'S GOBLET SQUATS – p.78 9 reps

3. PUSH-UPS – p.111 9 reps

**1. KETTLE BELL SWINGS –
p.125** 8 reps

**2. DAN JOHN'S GOBLET
SQUATS – p.78** 8 reps

3. PUSH-UPS – p.111
8 reps

**1. KETTLE BELL SWINGS –
p.125** 7 reps

**2. DAN JOHN'S GOBLET
SQUATS – p.78** 7 reps

3. PUSH-UPS – p.111
7 reps

**1. KETTLE BELL SWINGS –
p.125** 6 reps

**2. DAN JOHN'S GOBLET
SQUATS – p.78** 6 reps

3. PUSH-UPS – p.111
6 reps

DOWN TO

**1. KETTLE BELL SWINGS –
p.125** 1 reps

**2. DAN JOHN'S GOBLET
SQUATS – p.78** 1 rep

3. PUSH-UPS – p.111
1 rep

Cool down

Chapter 10

Quick fixes and feats of strength

The quick fix workouts are perfect for when you are short of time, or travelling and want to simply maintain your fitness levels or have a quick blast. Whilst in and of themselves, they will not be enough, they are short and tough, and can be done on their own or added on to the full programme, if you want to mix things up or add more intensity to the routines.

You should, of course still Warm-up before these quick fixes.

QUICK FIX WORKOUT 1

You will need: either a kettlebell or a dumbbell.
Duration: 10 minutes

1. KETTLEBELL SWINGS – p.125
Swing the bell for 20 seconds
Beginners use an 8kg, intermediates a 12kg and advanced a 16kg.

2. PUSH-UPS – p.111 – 6 reps
Rest till the top of the minute
Repeat for 10 rounds, with each round being 60 seconds.
Start swinging again at the top of every minute.

QUICK FIX WORKOUT 2: THE LEG CRANK

The leg crank is metabolic, great for strengthening the legs and getting that lean athletic look too!

Warm-up.

1. BODY WEIGHT SQUATS – p.71
12 reps

2. ANTERIOR LUNGES – p.97
12 reps each leg

3. POWER SKIPS – p.92
12 reps each leg

4. RICOCHETS – p.93
48 reps

5. SPILT JUMPS – p.118
12 reps

6 SQUAT JUMPS – p.119
12 reps

Gather yourself, and repeat the above circuit four to five times taking 15–20 minutes maximum.

Cool down.

QUICK FIX WORKOUT 3
Warm-up.

1. GRAVE DIGGERS – p.124
15 reps each side

2. CORE PUSH UPS – p.106
10 reps each side

3. REVERSE STEP UP – p.83
10 reps total

4. CRAWL – p.107
8 reps (2 steps forward, 2 steps back = 1)

QUICK FIX WORKOUT 4
Warm-up.

1. BOXING DRILLS TRIPLE PUNCH – p.73
30 reps to ceiling, 30 reps out in front, 30 reps to floor.

2. GRAVE DIGGERS – p.124
20 reps each side use shovel/spade or broom

3. JUMPING JACKS – p.82
30 reps

Repeat three times
Cool down 10 minutes.

Tests of strength and endurance

1. THE GET UP (SEE PAGE 108)

Often called the Turkish get up, this move is technically very tough and demanding which is why I have put it on its own. The benefits of this exercise are many, but I primarily use it as a way to get off the ground efficiently and to assess how the body moves. When you can perform the exercise in good form, it can be done for repetitions of up to say eight times on each side as a quick fix, or it can be added to the Pop-up routines themselves to add extra intensity.

2. THE PISTOL SQUAT (SEE PAGE 117)

Again, one of the most taxing of exercises, and only for the brave, attempt this after you can perform safely onto a low chair or box and ensure that you use correct form. Pistols don't suit people with existing knee problems, but for everyone else when performd correctly they help improve leg strength and power like no other move.

3. THE SINGLE ARM PUSH-UP (SEE PAGE 115)

The upper body equivalent of the pistol squat. Great because you can really increase maximum whole body strength without the need for any additional weight.

4. CHIN-UPS (SEE PAGE 105)

One of the toughest of the tough, demonstrated by good friends and top coaches Sonja Moses and Jos Thompson. Rule true girl power! Have fun with this exercise: chins, like so many types of exercise can be done outside and in different environments, but always ensure that your chosen bar/branch will take your weight.

Chapter 11
Clever strategies for fat loss

While the main focus of the Pop-up Gym is not weight loss per se, I recognise that it is a common goal for many. Therefore in this chapter I have hand-picked my favourite and most effective strategies to help you lose weight safely and effectively. Implement them gradually over time for more permanent weight management. However some of them are so effective that you will begin to notice the effects straight away.

I combine what I call 'stealth' training techniques, cutting-edge dietary advice and some new methods that I am sharing here for the first time. These have helped my clients to drop inches of their waistlines, shred body fat from key areas such as stomach and thighs and also given them new levels of vitality and mental strength.

1. WEIGH MORE NOT LESS

This is really cool. It's something I call 'stealth training' but one of my heroes, Bruce Lee, would have called it the art of 'training without training'. I have found that wearing a weighted jacket, even whilst walking around the house, helps you burn more calories, acting like an extra training session. Using a weighted jacket whilst training is one of the smartest ways to train as you can trick your body into working harder. I get my clients to wear one while doing the housework or going to the shops (worn under a t-shirt). The jacket cranks up your metabolism

helping you to burn more calories. Gradually build up to wearing the jacket for two hours with a 10–15lb (4.5–7kg) jacket. Use a loaded backpack if you can't buy a weighted jacket.

2. DO THE MATHS

Most 'experts' discourage frequent weighing on the basis of a number of unproven rationales. However, it has been shown that 75 per cent of successful dieters weigh themselves at least once per week, and 50 per cent do so daily. Those successful dieters said it helped them to pick up on the first signs of weight gain or change and that they were able to get back on track quicker.

Although I encourage my clients to 'do the maths', please note, I didn't say take your scales with you to the restaurant did I? Don't overdo it.

Even better is to have your body fat percentage measured to give you a more accurate breakdown of how much fat you need to drop and from where. You can do this at most good gyms and doctors or pharmacies. You can also buy these scales if you want to measure your body fat percentage at home.

3. FIDGET

I know it sounds a little weird but fidgeting can be a real calorie drain, and may use up to 1000kcal per day. *The Fidget Factor*, a little-known book by noted exercise physiologists Frank and Victor Katch, specifically explained the benefits of being just plain fidgety.

As far as examples, fidgeting constitutes just about anything other than watching television with a doughnut in one hand. So, if you like to paint, paint. If you like to clean your car every day, do it as every bit of movement counts.

New gadgets such as Nike's FuelBand, the Jawbone UP and others have devised ways of tracking activity levels, all of which can act as powerful motivators.

4. CONSISTENCY

I know it's boring, but this is the single most important variable of any training programme. It doesn't matter how hard you go or for how long, you have to be consistent. Fitness is one of the cornerstones to fat loss, and particularly, weight maintenance (once you've dropped the lard).

In the largest ongoing study of people who were trying to lose weight (more than 5,000 individuals), 94 per cent of those who succeeded in their goals consistently increased their physical activity levels. So that old maxim of 'little and often' is certainly better than 'once a blue moon'.

5. MAKE APPOINTMENTS

One of the most powerful motivators my clients talk about is having their exercise session in the diary. Now I know not everyone wants to hire a personal trainer (why not?) but there are ways to stick to a fitness programme nevertheless.

Even making an appointment with yourself by writing it down or making a date with a friend or work colleague greatly increases the likelihood of you sticking to your programme. Adherence and consistency go hand in hand. Give yourself no excuses.

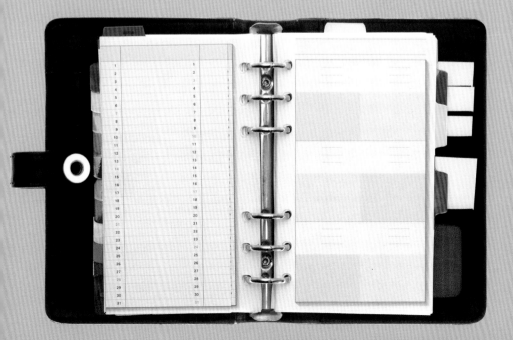

6. BIRDS OF A FEATHER STICK TOGETHER

A study of over 12,000 people across 32 years concluded that obesity
spreads through social ties. In other words, it may be that overweight
people tend to have pudgier friends. Pairs of friends and same sex siblings
tend to have the strongest effect on each other's weight loss. It works
a little like this: 'if my best mates and my brother are both overweight,
then perhaps it's OK for me to be overweight or gain a few pounds ...'
Whilst this is a controversial view, are there people in your life who are
frequently a negative influence on you and try to sabotage your weight
loss efforts?

My advice is to surround yourself by those who will have a good influence on your motivation, and give your willpower a fighting chance. To quote Muhammad Ali:

'You don't have to be what they want you to be: you're free to be what you want.'

7. GO GREEN!

Green tea that is … I believe green tea to be a genuine superfood.

There is an abundance of research around the health properties of green tea including its anti cancer, anti-oxidant and general health protective qualities.

It's in this chapter, however, because of its anti-obesity, and fat burning benefits. How? Well, there are sneaky, tiny extracts in tea called EGCG (epigallocatechin gallate) that increase the rate at which you burn calories and also burn fat via a number of pathways.

Aim for 500–1000mg per day – I tend to take mine earlier in the day.

8. THE ICE-MAN COMETH …

This is an unusual technique based on original research by NASA, and the research of a couple of super-smart scientists called Jack Kruse and Ray Kronise.

The theory here is that by manipulating body temperature (in this case making it cold) it forces the body to burn calories (from brown adipose tissue (BAT)) and maintain homeostasis. I've been using this technique with my athletes and clients for a year or two and have seen some great results, even when done in isolation (that is, without fitness training).

How does it work? I use this method in two ways:

<u>Method one</u> is to take a cold shower for five minutes with the water at the following temperatures and ratios: 20 seconds cold, 10 seconds room temperature.

Gradually build up to five minutes if you can.

<u>Method two</u> is to fill a basin with ice-cold water and put your feet in for up to 15 minutes.

Normally we advise this using this technique first thing in the morning, or at least earlier in the day – and it's definitely one for the brave and hardy among us.

9. GO (COCO) NUTS!

I am a big fan of VCO or virgin coconut oil, and I believe it should be part of your diet for a number of health-related reasons. I've included it in my fat loss section due to its ability to help you burn fat primarily by elevating your metabolism. VCO is very high in lauric acid; a medium chain fatty acid (MCT) found naturally only in coconuts and mothers' milk. Lauric acid has been shown to help the immune system through to

its antibacterial, antiviral and anti-microbial properties. Unlike other fats, MCTs are not easily stored in the body but instead are sent directly to the liver where they are converted into a usable energy source. It may also act as an appetite suppressant, helping you to feel fuller and prevent unhealthy snacking. The MCTs found in VCO are being used more and more by elite ultra-endurance athletes due to their metabolic efficiency and as an alternative to carbohydrates later on into these events. In many parts of the world it is also used to nourish and moisturise skin and hair

I suggest 'exchanging' other oils such as vegetable oils for VCO. I use it for roasting and frying on a medium-high heat. It's especially good in Asian dishes such as Thai curries. For more information go to **www.coconutology.com**

10. SMELLS A BIT FISHY! OMEGA 3S

I know it sounds counter intuitive, but it's true! Another kind of fat I recommend in the fight against fat are those found in fish oil, known as omega-3s. How? Basically omega-3s help to make cells more efficient at burning fat. Recent studies have shown that essential fatty acids can help control insulin and may also stimulate protein (muscle) synthesis. At the same time they direct other fatty acids in the body away from triglyceride synthesis (fat storage) and towards fatty acid oxidation. It's the active ingredients EPA (eicosapentaenoic acid) and DHA (docosahexaenoic acid) that are both long-chain fatty acids that make these great things happen. The richest sources of EPA and DHA in our diets come from cold-water fish. EPA and DHA are incorporated into cell membranes. While EPA is present in a variety of tissues, DHA is particularly concentrated in the brain and the retina. Clinical studies indicate that omega-3 supplementation may give a range of health benefits including brain and cognitive health, heart and cardiovascular health and anti-inflammatory properties. Whilst you can also get omega-3s from foods such as flax and chia seeds, those found in fish appear to be of greater value.

The next six months

Congratulations on completing the six-week Pop-up Gym challenge. You should be feeling fitter and leaner and enjoying all the benefits of improved health. However, your challenge doesn't need to stop here. The beauty of this programme is that you can use a technique called 'cycling' for as long as you like.

I suggest you take a rest week after week six to allow your body to regenerate, and then once you have done this you can go straight back to week two and repeat weeks three four, five and six. Every four weeks you should factor in a lighter rest week or a cardio week to allow your body to continue to progress.

The built-in variety of Pop-up Gym makes it a constant challenge for your muscles so they continue to reap the benefits from each successive cycle. Cycling the programme in this way really keeps your body guessing and the results coming. Remember to listen to your body and challenge yourself via the quick fixes and feats of strength, are you ready for your greatest challenge yet?

Setting benchmarks

Use the following form to record your results of the benchmark tests in Chapter 4 at the start of your programme and again after six weeks and six months.

WAIST TO HEIGHT RATIO

At start of programme	After six weeks	After six months
_____	_____	_____

THE ELEVATOR TEST

At start of programme	After six weeks	After six months
On the way down_5	On the way down_5	On the way down_5
On the way up_5	On the way up_5	On the way up_5

THE PLANK TEST

At start of programme	After six weeks	After six months
_____ mins	_____ mins	_____ mins

BODY WEIGHT

At start of programme	After six weeks	After six months
_____	_____	_____

RESTING HEART RATE (RHR)

At start of programme	After six weeks	After six months
_____	_____	_____

CIRCUMFERENCE MEASUREMENTS

At start of programme	After six weeks	After six months
Hips _____	Hips _____	Hips _____
Chest _____	Chest _____	Chest _____
Upper arm _____	Upper arm _____	Upper arm _____
Thigh _____	Thigh _____	Thigh _____

References

ON FITNESS

Exuberant Animal: *the power of health, play and joyful movement*, Frank Forencich, Authorhouse 2006

Facts and Fallacies of Fitness, Dr Mel C Siff, self-published, 1998

Spark!: *How exercise will improve the performance of your brain*, Dr John J. Ratey, Quercus, 2010

Survival of the Fittest, Mike Stroud, Yellow Jersey Press 2004

Ultimate Back Fitness and Performance, Dr Stuart McGill, Stuart McGill PhD, 2004 plus the DVD The Ultimate Back which covers McGill's techniques

ON NUTRITION

Essentials of Sports Nutrition and Supplements, Jose Antonio, Douglas Kalman, Jeffrey R. Stout and Mike Greenwood, Humana Press, 2008

Fats that Heal, Fats that Kill: *the complete guide to fats, oils, cholesterol and human health*, Dr Udo Erasmus, Alive Books 1993

Fist Full of Food, Matt Lovell, Buckingham Books, 2001

Fit Kids for Life: *a parent's guide to optimal nutrition and training for young athletes*, Jose Antonio and Jeffery Stout, Basic Health Publications 2004

Palm Sized Plan, Matt Lovell, Buckingham Book Publishing, 2011

ON MOTIVATION

Crucial Conversations: *tools for talking when stakes are high*, Kerry Patterson, Joseph Grenny, Ron McMillan and Al Switzler, McGraw Hill Professional, 2011

Influence: *the psychology of persuasion*, Robert B. Cialdini PhD, HarperBusiness, 2007

Learned Optimism: *how to change your mind and your life*, Martin E. P. Seligman PhD, Vintage Books USA, 2006

Progress Not Perfection: *your journey matters*, Kate Larsen, Expert Pub Inc, 2006

Switch: *how to change things when change is hard*, Chip and Dan Heath, Random House Business, 2011

The Corporate Athlete: *how to achieve maximal performance in business and life*, Jack Groppel, John Wiley & Sons, 2000

The Power of Less: *the 6 essential productivity principles that will change your life*, Leo Babauta, Hay House, 2009

Waistland: *the (r)evolutionary science behind our weight and fitness crisis*, Deirdre Barrett, W. W. Norton & Company, 2007.

Why Zebras Don't Get Ulcers, Robert M. Sapolsky, St Martin's Press, 2004

Willpower: *why self-control is the secret of success*, Roy F. Baumeister, Penguin, 2012

FOR FITNESS PROFESSIONALS

ACSM's Exercise is Medicine™: *a clinician's guide to exercise prescription*, Steven Jonas MD and Edward M Phillips, Lippincott Williams & Wilkins, 2009

Anatomy Trains: *myofascial meridians for manual and movement therapists*, Thomas W. Myers, Churchill Livingstone, 2014

Bad Science, Dr Ben Goldacre, Harper Perennial, 2009

High Performance Sports Conditioning, Bill Foran, Human Kinetics, 2001

Lifestyle Fitness Coaching, Dr James Gavin, Human Kinetics, 2005

Science and Practice of Strength Training, Vladimir M. Zatsiorsky and William J Kraemer, Human Kinetics, 2006

Secrets of Soviet Sports Fitness Training, Michael Yessis, William Morrow & Co, 1988

Sports Training Principles, Frank W. Dick, A&C Black, 2007

Strength & Conditioning: *biological principles and practical applications*, Marco Cardinale, Robert Newton and Kazunori Nosaka, Wiley-Blackwell, 2010

Supertraining, Yuri V Verkhoshansky, Mel C Siff and Michael Yessis, Verkhoshansky.com, 2009

The Naked Warrior, Pavel Tatsouline, Dragon Door Publications, 2003

Trick or Treatment: *the undeniable facts about alternative medicine*, Edzard Ernst and Simon Singh, W. W. Norton & Company, 2009

SELECTED WEB RESOURCES

American College of Sports Medicine *www.acsm.org*

Dan John *www.danjohn.net*

Dr Len Kravitz *www.drlenkravitz.com*

IDEA Health and Fitness Association *www.ideafit.com*

International Society of Sports Nutrition *www.sportsnutritionsociety.org*

Nike Training Club *www.nike.com/gb/en_gb/c/womens-training/apps/nike-training-club*

Sense About Science *www.senseaboutscience.org*

T-Tox *www.t-tox.com*

Tamaka Coconut Oil *www.coconutology.com*

Trigger Point Performance Therapy *www.tptherapy.com*

Wattbike *www.wattbike.com*

For specific references or further information please contact *info@popupgym.co.uk*

Benchmarks **32-45**, **136, 173**
Blood sugar levels **12**
Bone strength **12**

Circumference measurements **39**
Coaching yourself **26-28**
Cooling down, importance of **127**

Elevator test **35**
Energy bubble **31**
Energy levels **13**
EPOC **11**
Executive functioning **16**
Exercise
  and mental health **13, 14, 15**
  removing barriers to **18-23**
  and lifestyle **24-31**
Exercises **26-27, 67-125**
  Grey numbers show the full demonstration of the exercise
  Abdominal bracing **67, 131**
  Advanced medicine ball push-up **113**
  Anterior lunge **97, 144, 147, 151, 154, 160**
  Backpack clean **69, 144, 151**
  Band pull **120, 147, 154**
  Beginner pistol squat **116**
  Beginner push-up to row **102, 138, 142, 145, 150**
  Bent over row **70, 137, 141, 147, 154**
  Bodyweight kneeling push-up **101, 137, 141**
  Bodyweight squat **71, 137, 141, 144, 147, 151, 154, 160**
  Bodyweight hip raises **110, 128, 137, 141, 144, 151**
  Bottoms up shoulder press **104**
  Boxing **72, 161**

Bridge or plank **103, 137, 141**
Burpees **74, 144, 147, 151, 154**
Chain gang **76, 131**
Chin-up/pull-up **105, 163**
Core push-up **106, 147, 154, 161**
Crawl **107, 132, 161**
Dan John's goblet squat **78, 140, 156-7**
External leg rotation **77, 129**
Grave diggers **124, 161**
Heel to butt **79, 128, 144, 151**
High knee drill **80, 128, 144, 151**
Hip aeroplane **81, 138, 142, 145, 150**
Internal leg rotation **68, 129**
Jumping Jack **82, 142, 145, 149, 150, 153, 156-7, 161**
Kettle bell get up **108, 162**
Kettle bell swings **125, 149, 153, 156-7, 159**
Lateral lunge **84, 138, 142, 145, 150**
Leg control **86**
March on the spot **87, 128, 129, 137, 138, 141**
Medicine ball push-up **112, 147, 154**
Medicine ball straight chop **88, 128, 140, 147**
Medicine ball wood chop **89, 140, 154**
Mid range rotation with medicine ball **100, 147, 154**
Mountain climber **114, 140, 147, 154**
Pistol squat **117, 162**
Pop-up **90, 149, 153, 156**
Power skip **92, 138, 142, 144, 145, 147,**

150, 151, 154, 160
Push-up **111, 140, 144, 149, 151, 153, 156, 159**
Reverse step-up **83, 161**
Ricochet **93, 160**
Rotational step-up **85, 150**
Side plank rotation **121, 140**
Single arm push-up **115, 163**
Single leg dead lift balance **94, 140**
Single leg kick **95**
Split jump **118, 147, 160**
Squat jump **119, 147, 154, 160**
Step up **96, 138, 142, 145**
Superman **123, 133, 137, 141**
Swiss ball 'stir the pot' **120, 138, 142, 145, 150**
Triple punch with dumbbell **98**
Walk out **122, 129**

Fat loss **164-171**
  Appointments **167**
  Consistency **167**
  Fidgeting **166**
  Green tea **169**
  Ice baths **169**
  Virgin coconut oil (VCO) **171**
  Weighing yourself **166**
  Weighted jacket **165**
Feats of strength **162-163**
Food **29, 53**

Habits **47, 49**
Half waist to height ratio **33**
Heart health **13**
High-intensity training **135**

Immune system **17**
Interval training **135**

Longevity **17**

Metabolic rate **11**
Motivation **46-55**
Perceived rate of exertion **42-43**
Plank test **36**
Pop-up promises **54-55**
Power coaching questions **48**
Preparatory exercises **131-133**

Recovery **30**
Resting heart rate (RHR) **38**

Sleep **17**
Stress **14, 23, 29**
Stretching **58-59**
  Active stretching **58**
  Butt and gluteal fascial release **63**
  Child's pose **60**
  Dynamic stretching **58**
  Fascial release **59**
  Hamstrings **61**
  IT band fascial release **64**
  Lower limbs/calves **62**
  Medicine ball chop and lift **65**
  Pectoral fascial release **63**
  Piriformis/butt stretch **64**
  Plantar fascia release **62**
  Static stretching **58**
  Step and twist **60**
  Trigger points **59**
Suppleness **56-65**

Visualisation **51-52**

Warm-up drills **128-130**
Warming up **40, 127**
Weight (see also fat loss)
  finding a healthy weight **38**
  maintaining **12**
Will power **50**
Workouts **134-157**
  Quick fix workouts **158-161**

Acknowledgments

Firstly, to all of my clients, my desire for your success grows ever stronger.

To the health educators, academics and mentors who have influenced me over the years in particular Dr Mel Siff who made me question the fitness status quo, and changed the way I think (didn't?), to Dr Len Kravitz who is a true teacher and Kate Larsen, who opened my eyes to coaching.

To the coaches I'm grateful to work alongside, in particular Pete Williams and Gary Stebbing, who continue to share with me with their thirst to grow, kaizen boys.

To the Club 51 team, thank you for your support and dedication.

To my superb fitness models and fellow coaches: Sonja Moses, Joslyn Thompson Rule, Jamie Stumpe, Monika Mikalauskaite and Seb Hicks.

To Lisa and my team at Bloomsbury Publishing, my agent Diana at Rupert Heath and my friends at W Communications.

To my family for their support and love.

To my best mate Barry for telling me it how it is oh, and the TW1 (and 2!) crew.

And of course, to my wife Jo, my best friend and greatest support.

Picture credits

All photographs by Gerard Brown except as follows:

Shutterstock: 10 Bikerider London; 12 Dim Dimich; 13 t DKVector, b Deepblue-Photograph er; 15 EtiAmmos; 16 Ken Tannenbaum; 18 Pete Saloutos; 19 Croisy; 20 Dragon Images; 22 Peter Bernik; 24 Dotshock; 27 Danil Nevsky; 29 Miguel Garcia Saavedra; 30 Racorn; 31 Dmitrij Skorobogatov; 32 Mezzotint; 34 Val Lawless; 39 Anna Rassadnikova; 42 Anchiy; 45 Jarous; 46 FCG; 47 Paula French; 49 Ditty_about_summer; 53 Shaiith; 56 Spwidoff; 57 l Alexander Yakovlev, r Ivan Pavlisko, b Markus Gann; 135 l Garsya, c Perig, r AlenD; 136 l Deymos Photo, c Brostock, r Africa Studio; 164 Alekso 94; 166 Cretolamna; 167 Sergey Karpov; 168 Monkey Business Images; 169 Pullia; 171 Marco Mayer.

Club 51: 61r; 64b; 104